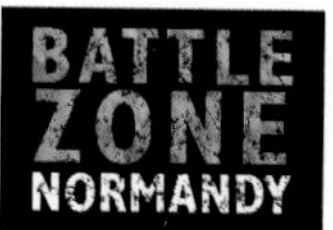

OPERATION EPSOM

The 'Battle Zone Normandy' Series

Orne Bridgehead Lloyd Clark

Sword Beach Ken Ford

Juno Beach Ken Ford

Gold Beach Simon Trew

Omaha Beach Stephen Badsey & Tim Bean

Utah Beach Stephen Badsey

Villers-Bocage George Forty

Battle for Cherbourg R.P.W. Havers

Operation Epsom Lloyd Clark

Battle for St-Lô Nigel de Lee

Battle for Caen Simon Trew & Stephen Badsey

Operation Cobra Christopher Pugsley

Road to Falaise Stephen Hart

Falaise Pocket Paul Latawski

All of these titles can be ordered via the
Sutton Publishing website
www.suttonpublishing.co.uk

The 'Battle Zone Normandy'
Editorial and Design Team

Series Editor Simon Trew

Senior Commissioning Editor Jonathan Falconer

Assistant Editor Nick Reynolds

Cover and Page Design Martin Latham

Editing and Layout Donald Sommerville

Mapping Map Creation Ltd

Photograph Scanning and Mapping Bow Watkinson

Index Michael Forder

BATTLE ZONE NORMANDY

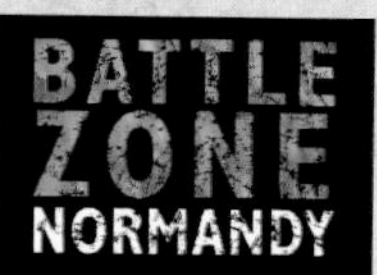

OPERATION EPSOM

LLOYD CLARK

Series Editor: Simon Trew

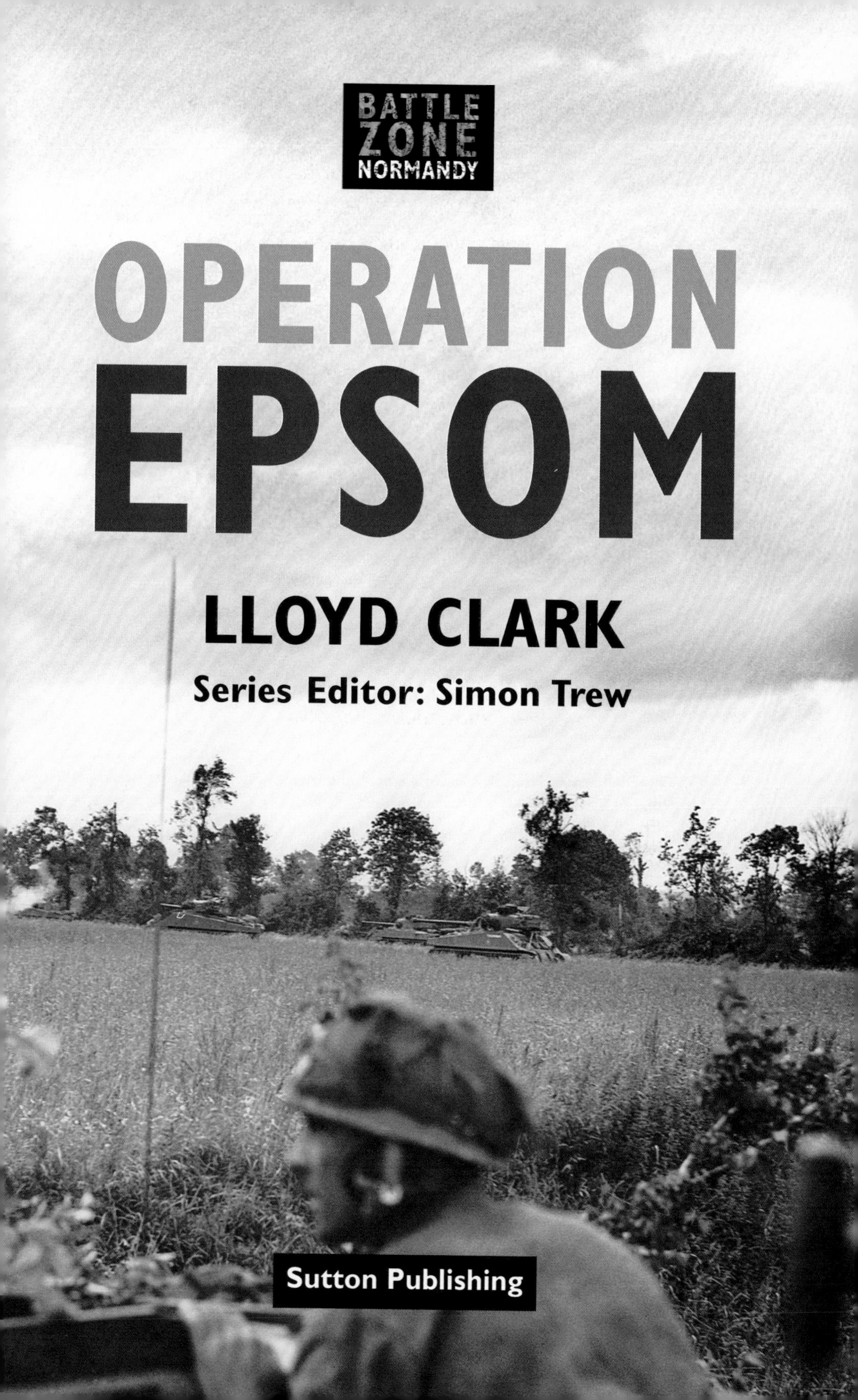

Sutton Publishing

First Published in 2004 by
Sutton Publishing Limited · Phoenix Mill
Thrupp · Stroud · Gloucestershire · GL5 2BU

British Library Cataloguing in Publication Data
A catalogue record for this book is available from The British Library.

ISBN 0-7509-3008-X

Typeset in 10.5/14 pt Sabon

Printed and bound in England by
J.H. Haynes & Co. Ltd, Sparkford

Front cover: A Churchill tank of 7th Royal Tank Regiment and men of 8th Royal Scots on 28 June. *(Imperial War Museum [IWM] B6124)*

Page 1: The Hill 112 memorial, looking in the direction of Baron-sur-Odon and Grainville-sur-Odon (on the horizon). *(Author)*

Page 3: Sherman tanks of 29th Armoured Brigade engaging German positions near Cheux on 26 June. *(IWM B5977)*

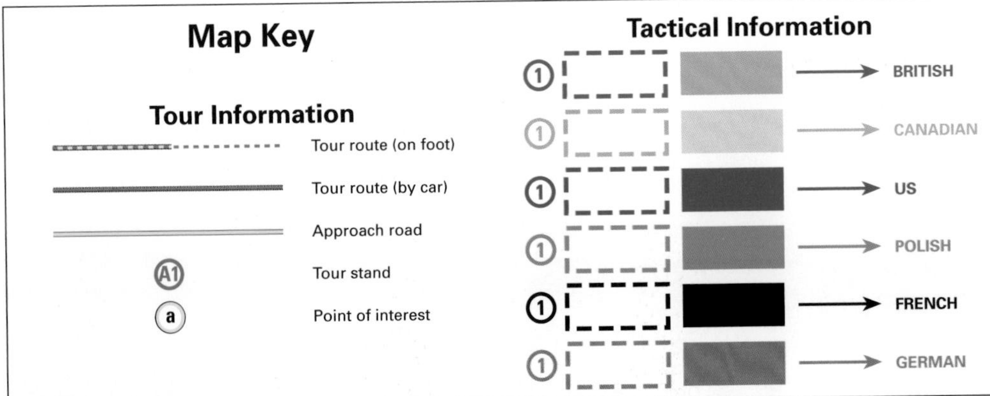

CONTENTS

THE NORMANDY BATTLEFIELD

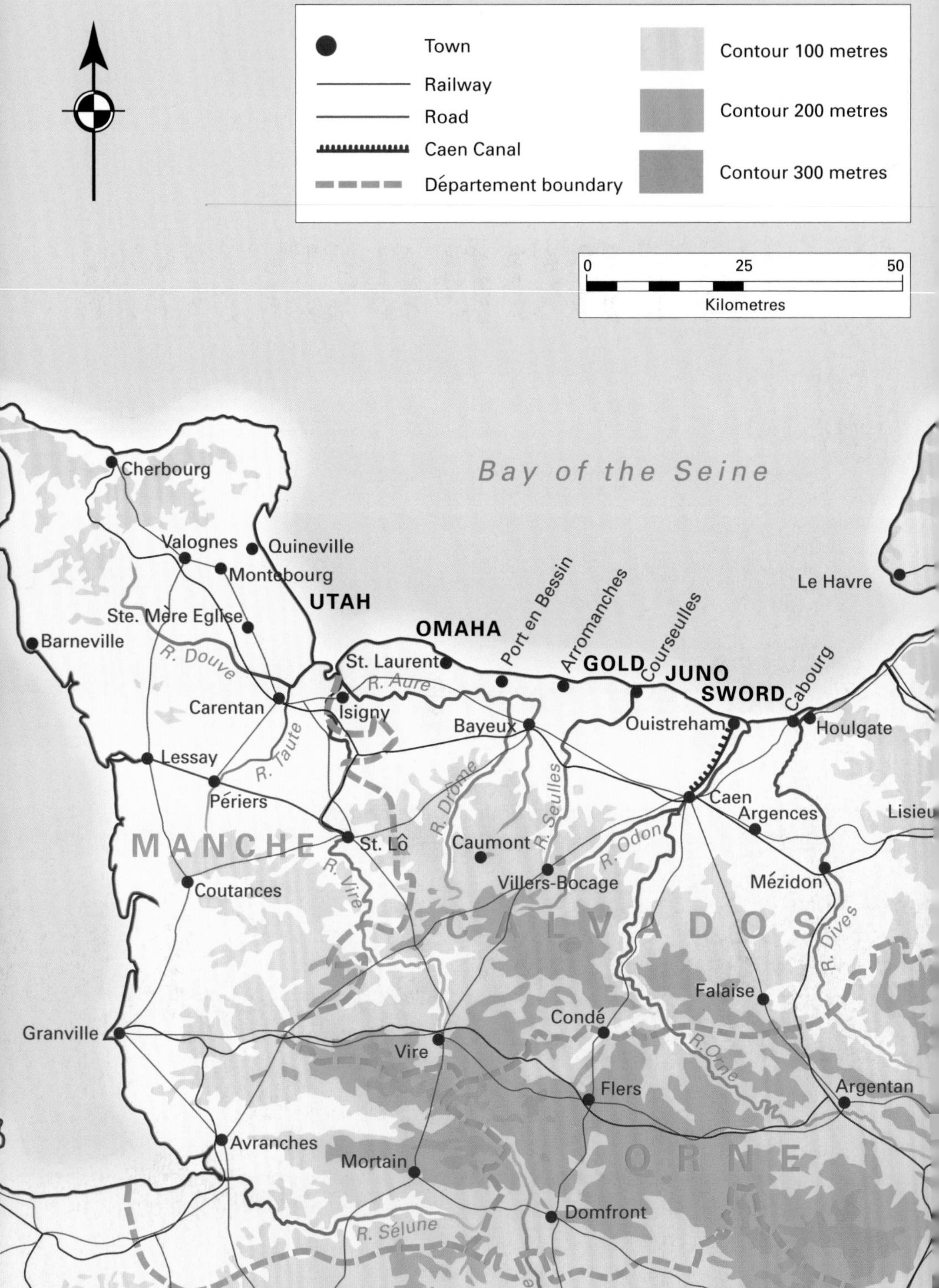

PART ONE

INTRODUCTION

BATTLE ZONE NORMANDY

The Battle of Normandy was one of the greatest military clashes of all time. From late 1943, when the Allies appointed their senior commanders and began the air operations that were such a vital preliminary to the invasion, until the end of August 1944, it pitted against one another several of the most powerful nations on earth, as well as some of their most brilliant minds. When it was won, it changed the world forever. The price was high, but for anybody who values the principles of freedom and democracy, it is difficult to conclude that it was one not worth paying.

I first visited Lower Normandy in 1994, a year after I joined the War Studies Department at the Royal Military Academy Sandhurst (RMAS). With the 50th anniversary of D-Day looming, it was decided that the British Army would be represented at several major ceremonies by one of the RMAS's officer cadet companies. It was also suggested that the cadets should visit some of the battlefields, not least to bring home to them the significance of why they were there. Thus, at the start of June 1994, I found myself as one of a small team of military and civilian directing staff flying with the cadets in a draughty and noisy Hercules transport to visit the beaches and fields of Calvados, in my case for the first time.

I was hooked. Having met some of the veterans and seen the ground over which they fought – and where many of their friends died – I was determined to go back. Fortunately, the Army encourages battlefield touring as part of its soldiers' education, and on numerous occasions since 1994 I have been privileged to return to Normandy, often to visit new sites. In the process I have learned a vast amount, both from my colleagues (several of whom are contributors to this series) and from my enthusiastic and sometimes tri-service audiences, whose professional insights and penetrating questions have frequently made me re-examine my own assumptions and prejudices. Perhaps inevitably, especially when standing in one of Normandy's beautifully-

Above: Men of 6th Royal Scots Fusiliers advance through the mist and smoke that masked their attack at 0730 hours on 26 June. *(IWM B5953)*

Page 7: Sherman tanks of 23rd Hussars moving up to the front line just after dawn on 26 June at the start of Operation Epsom. *(IWM B6142)*

maintained Commonwealth War Graves Commission cemeteries, I have also found myself deeply moved by the critical events that took place there in the summer of 1944.

'Battle Zone Normandy' was conceived by Jonathan Falconer, Commissioning Editor at Sutton Publishing, in 2001. Why not, he suggested, bring together recent academic research – some of which challenges the general perception of what happened on and after 6 June 1944 – with a perspective based on familiarity with the ground itself? We agreed that the opportunity existed for a series that would set out to combine detailed and accurate narratives, based mostly on primary sources, with illustrated guides to the ground itself, which could be used either in the field (sometimes quite literally), or by the armchair explorer. The book in your hands is the product of that agreement.

The 'Battle Zone Normandy' series consists of 14 volumes, covering most of the major and many of the minor engagements that went together to create the Battle of Normandy. The first six

THE NORMANDY BATTLEFIELD, MID-JUNE TO MID-JULY

Allied front line, evening 12 June

Contour 50 metres

Contour 100 metres

Contour 200 metres

Inundated area

0 10 20

Kilometres

CAP DE LA HAGUE
Auderville
CAP LÉVI
POINTE DE BARFLEUR
CHERBOURG
St-Pierre-Église
Barfleur
Beaumont-Hague
Tourlaville
Quettehou
St-Vaast-la-Hougue
Delasse
CAP DE FLAMANVILLE
les Pieux
VALOGNES
Quinéville
Bricquebec
Montebourg
R. Merderet
R. Douve
Orglandes
Ste-Mère-Église
St-Sauveur-le-Vicomte
Barneville
Pont-l'Abbé
Chef-du-Pont
CAP DE CARTERET
St-Lô-d'Ourville
Bay of the Seine
Grandcamp-les-Bains
Vierville-sur-Mer
Arromanches-les-Bains
Port-en-Bessin
Courseulles-sur-Mer
CABOURG
la Haye-du-Puits
Carentan
Isigny
R. Aure
Montmartin-en-Graignes
BESSIN
BAYEUX
Lion-sur-Mer
Ouistreham
R. Seulles
le Molay-Littry
Lessay
Périers
R. Taute
St-Jean-de-Daye
R. Vire
St-Clair-sur-l'Elle
R. Drome
Trungy
Cambes
R. Orne
Hérouvillette
Pont-Hébert
Villiers-Fossard
Balleroy
Tilly-sur-Seulles
Carpiquet
CAEN
St-Manvieu
Troarn
R. Dives
BOCAGE
St-Sauveur-Lendelin
Marigny
Berigny
Hottot-les-Bagues
Cagny
ST-LÔ
Noyers-Bocage
R. Odon
Caumont
Vimont
COUTANCES
Condé-sur-Vire
Villers-Bocage
Évrecy
May-sur-Orne
Torigni-sur-Vire
Bretteville-sur-Laize

The 49th Division memorial on the D139 Fontenay-le-Pesnel to Rauray road, on the western flank of the Epsom battlefield. *(Author)*

books deal with the airborne and amphibious landings on 6 June 1944, and with the struggle to create the firm lodgement that was the prerequisite for eventual Allied victory. Five further volumes cover some of the critical battles that followed, as the Allies' plans unravelled and they were forced to improvise a battle very different from that originally intended. Finally, the last three titles in the series examine the fruits of the bitter attritional struggle of June and July 1944, as the Allies irrupted through the German lines or drove them back in fierce fighting. The series ends, logically enough, with the devastation of the German armed forces in the 'Falaise Pocket' in late August.

Whether you use these books while visiting Normandy, or to experience the battlefields vicariously, we hope you will find them as interesting to read as we did to research and write. Far from the inevitable victory that is sometimes represented, D-Day and the ensuing battles were full of hazards and unpredictability. Contrary to the view often expressed, had the invasion failed, it is far from certain that a second attempt could have been mounted. Remember this, and the significance of the contents of this book, not least for your life today, will be the more obvious.

Dr Simon Trew
Royal Military Academy Sandhurst
December 2003

ACKNOWLEDGEMENTS

There are many people whom I would like to thank for their help in researching this book, but I must stress that any mistakes in it are mine and mine alone: the team at Sutton Publishing, as usual, have been a joy to work with, and in particular Jonathan Falconer and Nick Reynolds; Dr Simon Trew, the series editor, who has been an inspiration throughout, whilst Andrew Orgill, John Pearce and Ken Franklin at the Central Library, Royal Military Academy Sandhurst, have always gone out of their way to make the job of a researcher that much easier with their affability, knowledge, and professionalism.

I should also like to thank the staffs at the National Archives (formerly the Public Record Office), Kew; the Departments of Documents, Books and Photographs at the Imperial War Museum; the National Army Museum; the Institute of Historical Research, the University of London; the Liddell Hart Centre for Military Archives, King's College, London; and Mr Sydney Jary MC and Mr Ernst Steiner, veterans of the fighting on and near Hill 112 in the summer of 1944, for their valuable insights into the terrain, fighting methods and weaponry employed by both sides during this period. My friends, colleagues and students at the Royal Military Academy, both military and civilian, have also been immensely helpful throughout the research and writing of this book.

As always, I should like to thank my family for their forbearance at having to live with an author: Catriona, Freddie, Charlotte and Henry – thank you. Finally, I would like to dedicate this book to my sister-in-law, Caroline, and my brother, Brent, in recognition of their great strength in the face of adversity.

Lloyd Clark
RMA Sandhurst
February 2004

PART TWO

HISTORY

CHAPTER 1

THE SITUATION AND PRELIMINARY ATTACKS

Operation 'Epsom' is not the most famous of the Normandy battles, but it was an important battle in the summer of 1944. The events of 6 June have naturally captured the public imagination, but as the fighting thereafter has perhaps been perceived to lack the drama of the initial landings, it has not become vigorous in the collective popular consciousness. This does not, of course, mean that operations after D-Day were militarily insignificant; indeed, Operation Epsom was central to the unfolding Normandy campaign and continues to raise significant questions about Allied strategy, the conduct of British operations and the combat effectiveness of the German forces. Nevertheless, popular understanding about the battle is almost non-existent and those with some knowledge often have a jaundiced view as a result of the fervour that continues to surround assessments of General Montgomery's role and achievements as Allied Land Forces Commander. One argument reasons that Epsom failed in its overt and tacit objectives, while another believes that the operation achieved exactly the sort of strategic impact that it was designed to achieve. This book seeks to cast some light on these arguments but, more

Above: Lt Gen Omar N. Bradley, commander of First US Army in Normandy, listens patiently to Field Marshal Sir Alan Brooke, British Chief of the Imperial General Staff, in March 1945. *(IWM BU2237)*

Page 13: 15th Division attacks towards the Villers-Bocage–Caen road on 28 June with Churchill tanks in support. *(IWM B6118)*

Monty and his commanders on 22 June. *Front row (l to r):* Maj-Gen G.I. Thomas, 43rd Division; Lt-Gen G.C. Bucknall, XXX Corps; Lt-Gen H.D.G. Crerar, First (Canadian) Army; General B.L. Montgomery, 21st Army Group; Lt-Gen M.C. Dempsey, Second (British) Army; Air Vice Marshal H. Broadhurst, 83 Group RAF; Lt-Gen N.M. Ritchie, XII Corps. *Middle row:* Maj-Gen D.C. Bullen-Smith, 51st Division; Maj-Gen R.F.L. Keller, 3rd Canadian Division; Maj-Gen D.A.H. Graham, 50th Division; Maj-Gen G.P.B. Roberts, 11th Armoured Division; Lt-Gen R.N. O'Connor, VIII Corps; Maj-Gen E.H. Barker, 49th Division; Lt-Gen J.T. Crocker, I Corps. *Back row:* Maj-Gen G.H.A. MacMillan, 15th Division; Maj-Gen R.N. Gale, 6th Airborne Division; Maj-Gen C. Foulkes, 2nd Canadian Division. (IWM B5916)

fundamentally, tries to tell the story of what actually happened on the Epsom battlefield during that week in June 1944 when the British forces launched the largest Allied offensive since D-Day and the Germans, already stretched and weary but preparing a massive armoured counter-stroke themselves, had to react swiftly lest the British dislodge the cornerstone of their defences.

The Background to Operation Epsom

There is still considerable controversy surrounding Montgomery's strategy in Normandy and, therefore, what Operation Epsom was actually designed to achieve. Opinion is concentrated into two main camps, the apologists and the critics, which are largely inhabited by British and American historians respectively. The apologists

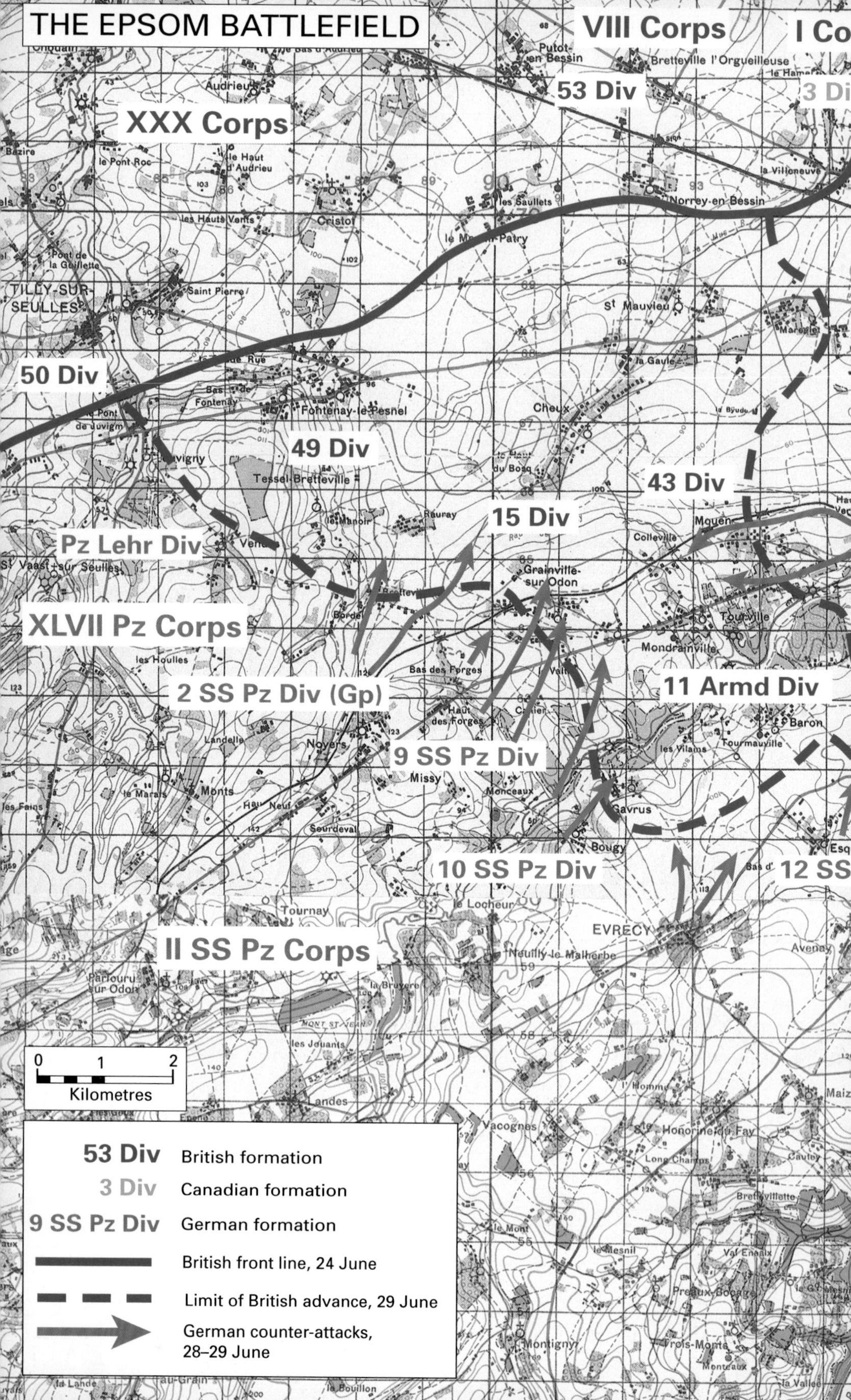
THE EPSOM BATTLEFIELD
VIII Corps
I Co
53 Div
3 Di
XXX Corps
50 Div
49 Div
43 Div
15 Div
Pz Lehr Div
XLVII Pz Corps
2 SS Pz Div (Gp)
11 Armd Div
9 SS Pz Div
10 SS Pz Div
12 SS
II SS Pz Corps
Audrieu
Putot-en-Bessin
Bretteville l'Orgueilleuse
le Haut d'Audrieu
le Pont Roc
Bazire
Cristot
les Hauts Vents
les Saullets
le Mesnil-Patry
Norrey-en-Bessin
la Villeneuve
TILLY-SUR-SEULLES
Saint Pierre
St Mauvieu
Marcelet
la Gaule
Fontenay-le-Pesnel
Bas de Fontenay
Cheux
le Pont de Juvigny
Juvigny
Tessel-Bretteville
le Haut du Bosq
le Manoir
Rauray
Mouen
Colleville
Vendes
St Vaast-sur-Seulles
Grainville-sur-Odon
Tourville
Mondrainville
les Houlles
Bas des Forges
Haut des Forges
Baron
Tourmauville
les Vilains
Landelle
Noyers
Missy
le Marais
Monts
Monceaux
Gavrus
Bougy
Seurdeval
Tournay
le Locheur
EVRECY
Neuilly-le-Malherbe
Avenay
Parfouru-sur-Odon
la Bruyère
les Jouants
Landes
Vacognes
Ste Honorine-du-Fay
Long Champs
Bretteville
le Mont
le Mesnil
Val Ennelix
Préaux-Bocage
Montigny
Trois-Monts
Monteaux
la Vallée
le Bouillon
la Lande
0
1
2
Kilometres
53 Div
British formation
3 Div
Canadian formation
9 SS Pz Div
German formation
British front line, 24 June
Limit of British advance, 29 June
German counter-attacks, 28–29 June

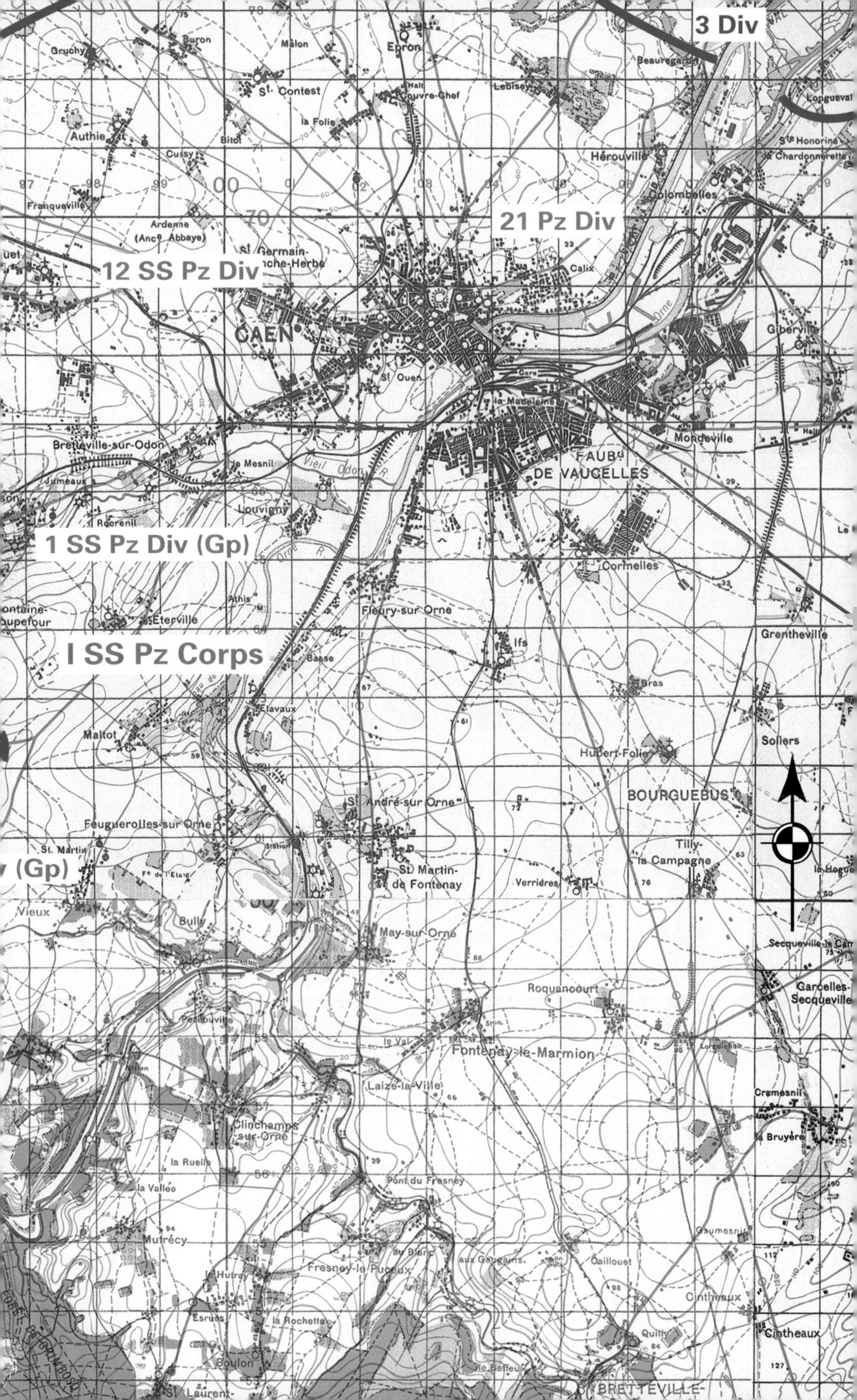
3 Div
21 Pz Div
12 SS Pz Div
1 SS Pz Div (Gp)
I SS Pz Corps
(Gp)
CAEN
FAUBG DE VAUCELLES
BOURGUEBUS
Colombelles
Mondeville
Cormelles
Fleury-sur-Orne
Ifs
Bras
Hubert-Folie
Soliers
Grentheville
Tilly-la Campagne
Verrières
St. Martin-de Fontenay
St. André-sur Orne
May-sur-Orne
Fontenay-le-Marmion
Roquancourt
Garcelles-Secqueville
Maltot
Eterville
Louvigny
Bretteville-sur-Odon
Carpiquet
Authie
Buron
Gruchy
St. Contest
Epron
Lebisey
Hérouville
Giberville
Feuguerolles-sur Orne
Clinchamps-sur-Orne
Laize-la-Ville
Fresney-le-Puceux
Cintheaux
Quilly
BRETTEVILLE-

A piper leads 2nd Argyll and Sutherland Highlanders forward to the battalion's forming-up area on the afternoon of 25 June. *(IWM B5988)*

accept Montgomery's post-war statements that Caen was an important, but not essential objective during June and early July. Thus, although the plan to take Caen on D-Day failed, as did subsequent attempts to isolate the city, because the strategic landscape changed and competing demands on resources developed, this did not matter. Montgomery did recognise, however, that the Germans believed the city to be critical to their Normandy front and, therefore, if he put pressure on it he would draw German forces away from the Americans. At a conference at his tactical headquarters in Creully on the evening of 22 June at which all Second (British) Army's corps and divisional commanders were in attendance, Montgomery said, 'We have been successful in pulling the German reserves to the CAEN, or eastern, sector of our lodgement area. This has relieved pressure in the American sector, and as a result we now own the whole of the Cherbourg peninsula except the port of Cherbourg itself.' He went on to say that

Lieutenant General Omar Bradley's First US Army would take Cherbourg soon and then, with the Allies all facing the same way, the Americans would take Brittany as long as the British continued to draw the Germans from them. This, Montgomery insisted, was always the plan.

The critics, on the other hand, believe that Caen was vital and could have been taken far earlier than it was, had it not been for the lacklustre performance of Montgomery and the Anglo-Canadian army. This school of thought argues that Montgomery did think that Caen was essential and that he revised his opinion only as a result of his inability to seize the city in the first weeks of the campaign. The same can be said for his desire to take the pressure off the Americans which, they insist, was most definitely not the plan. In reality the plan was for the break-out from Normandy to come from the left, from Montgomery on the shortest route to Paris. Moreover, far from Montgomery magnetising German armour to the east by his offensive actions, these formations would have ended up there anyway as they were preparing for a counter-stroke against Bayeux. Indeed, once the Americans looked certain to take Cherbourg and were looking to break out towards Brittany, the British had no option but to force Caen. Thus, Montgomery contrived a version of reality that glossed over his own failure and made Epsom look part of a preconceived plan.

The polarities of the arguments outlined above are probably both misguided and do no justice to the complexity of the situation facing Montgomery and his troops during June 1944. There were many pressures pushing down on Montgomery during this period to 'make progress' as the Anglo-Canadians had not taken as much territory as had been expected in the first two weeks of the fighting and Caen was still in German hands. Thus, Montgomery combined the need to try and take Caen and provide room for the ever growing number of Allied troops, with his desire – newly conceived or not – to fix the Germans in the east and, thus, Operation Epsom was born. Epsom, Montgomery understood, would have to be a major offensive if his ambitions were to be successful due to the strength of the forces facing him and the nature of the terrain and, as was his wont, he decided to build up 'overwhelming' strength for the attack. Nevertheless, time was not on his side; with every passing day, questions were being asked by politicians and his military colleagues about the lack of progress, and the Germans were being given an opportunity to develop their defences and reinforce.

A Universal Carrier on the Epsom battlefield during the battle. The carrier had rests for Bren guns and a Boys anti-tank rifle (hence it is commonly known as the Bren gun carrier). It was usually used to transport heavy weapons and stores, or to evacuate wounded. *(IWM B5990)*

THE BIRTH OF OPERATION EPSOM

The conception of the operation that was to grow into Epsom was announced in a directive Montgomery issued to his army commanders on 18 June. In this he outlined the need for Lieutenant-General (Lt-Gen) Sir Miles Dempsey, commander of Second (British) Army, to 'capture Caen... as the first step in the full development of our plans' while the Americans took Cherbourg. The initial aim was for a pincer movement from both flanks against Caen with British I and XXX Corps attacking to the west of the city for four days, followed by the main attack delivered by British VIII Corps east of the River Orne on 22 June. It soon became clear, however, that a corps could not assemble in the tight Orne bridgehead. Thus, on 19 June, Montgomery announced that the left wing of the pincer would be formed by the troops of I Corps already there, whilst VIII Corps was to be 'switched to form part of the right, or western wing of the pincer movement'. In more detail, the bridgehead east of Caen was to be extended by 51st (Highland) Division in order to force the Germans to commit 21st Panzer Division and its reserves to the area. Following this, to the west of Caen, VIII Corps would be launched in an attack across the Odon and the Orne to Bretteville-sur-Laize. This attack would be supported on the right flank by a preliminary advance, to be made by XXX Corps and led by 49th (West Riding) Division, supported by 8th Armoured Brigade, to secure the high ground from Rauray to Noyers-Bocage, known as Operation 'Martlet'. On the left of the attack, I Corps was to capture Carpiquet airfield as the offensive progressed. However, even as the commanders began their planning following Montgomery's demands, nature intervened and a storm lashed into Normandy.

The Great Storm 19–22 June 1944

Daily average landed	*Men*		*Vehicles*		*Stores (tons)*	
	British	*US*	*British*	*US*	*British*	*US*
15–18 June	15,774	18,938	2,965	2,929	10,666	14,308
19–22 June	3,982	5,865	1,375	1,051	4,286	3,064

Source: Ellis, *Victory in the West*, p. 274.

The Great Storm, as it became known, lasted for three days and upset Allied efforts to put men, equipment, vehicles and stores ashore. Nevertheless, the situation would have been far more serious had it not been for the 'Gooseberry' breakwaters and the 'Mulberry' harbours, as these enabled the logistic effort to continue in spite of the weather. Even so, the storm did hamper Montgomery's build-up for Operation Epsom.

On 20 June, Montgomery wrote to General Simpson in the War Office:

'The weather is still the very devil. A gale all day yesterday; the same today... In particular I must have 43d Division complete and more artillery ammunition... The real point is that the delay imposed on us by the weather is just what the enemy needs, i.e. time to get more divisions over here and we know some more are on the move. It is all a very great nuisance.'

Source: Nigel Hamilton, *Monty: Master of the Battlefield*, p. 682.

The result was that Operation Epsom had to be postponed and so the limited attack out of the Orne bridgehead was rearranged for 23 June, Operation Martlet for 25 June and Epsom for 26 June. The delay gave the British the time that they required to mount the attack but, of course, it also gave the Germans time to move resources to Normandy without Allied aircraft devastating their efforts, as they were grounded by the extraordinary mid-summer conditions. A German counter-attack at this point would, as *SS-Sturmbannführer* (Major) Hubert Meyer, Chief of Staff, 12th SS Panzer Division *Hitlerjugend*, has said, have 'caught the enemy at a moment of extraordinary weakness', but he also commented that, 'the race to assemble had already been lost.' In the event, the German attack was not ready, and the Allies were about to unleash a storm of their own that, Montgomery hoped, the Germans would not be able to withstand.

The Mulberry harbour near Arromanches after the Great Storm. *(IWM B6064)*

THE TERRAIN

Operation Epsom was developed with the strengths of the defenders and the nature of the terrain in mind, although the final plan rather underestimated the neutralising effect of both. The ground over which the attack was to take place was fertile cultivated countryside

A narrow road bordered by a stout hedgerow and robust farm buildings at la Gaule, features typical of the *bocage* countryside of Normandy. *(Author)*

so typical of Normandy. The most northerly section, the first to be crossed by the British attack, was made up of hedgeless fields up to the insignificant Mue stream. Next were some ridges or spurs emanating from high ground to the south-west. On the XXX Corps front, spurs ran north to Fontenay-le-Pesnel and to the north-east via Brettevillette to Rauray. From here the high ground extended east to le Haut du Bosq (marked simply as le Bosq on modern maps) on the VIII Corps' front and continued in that direction until it petered out to the south of Cheux. Further south, another spur ran off north-east from Noyers-Bocage to Grainville-sur-Odon. In this area there was good defensive *bocage* countryside characterised by small fields rimmed with thick and steeply embanked hedges and sunken roads, containing small stout farms with neighbouring woods and orchards in a broken landscape. Studded with small villages, ideal for defensive strongpoints, the ground then fell away to the valley of the Odon which was covered in thick woods. The

Odon was a minor river that in itself was not a significant obstacle, but in places its banks were extremely steep and there were few bridges. Beyond the river and the woods on its southern side was the high ground of Hills 112 and 113, from which Caen could be seen on a clear day just 10 kilometres (km) to the north-east, the British start line a similar distance to the north, the Rauray ridge 8 km to the north-west and the southern approaches to Caen and the River Orne 6 km to the south-east. To reach the Orne, a more substantial river than the Odon, a series of ridges and more *bocage* had to be crossed, but beyond it was open country leading to Bretteville-sur-Laize, some 13 km south of Caen.

The vital artery into Cheux from the northern part of the Epsom battlefield. *(Author)*

THE GERMANS

Defending the front that was to be attacked by VIII Corps was 12th SS Panzer Division *Hitlerjugend*, with elements of 21st Panzer Division to its east and elements of Panzer Lehr Division to its west. These divisions were the constituent parts of I SS Panzer Corps, which had been created in July 1943 (less 21st Panzer Division which was a more recent addition) and was commanded by *SS-Obergruppenführer* (Lt-Gen) Josef 'Sepp' Dietrich. The corps had been holding the area for nearly three weeks, knew the ground intimately and had well-prepared defences, with its infantry well dug-in, machine guns skilfully positioned, observation points carefully selected, vehicles and anti-tank guns expertly camouflaged and minefields laid in some areas. 12th SS Panzer Division had been formed mainly from the *Hitlerjugend* youth movement during the spring of 1943 but was strengthened by some experienced soldiers who had served with either the German Army or 1st SS Panzer Division *Leibstandarte*. A little more than a year after its formation it was in Normandy and had suffered quite a battering in the first two weeks of the fighting there. By the time that Epsom was launched the division, commanded by *SS-Standartenführer* (Colonel) Kurt Meyer, looked drastically under strength on paper and Meyer says in his memoirs that the division was already 'surviving at subsistence levels', but in fact the reality was considerably different. It is true that the division was short of infantry, but on 25 June it had 58 Panzer IVs and 44 Panthers with another 18 Panzer IV tanks and 10 Panthers under repair and soon to be returned to operational status. The division also had 233 half-tracks and scout cars available with some 17 combat-ready

British 5.5-inch gun firing in support of 15th Division's attack on 26 June. *(IWM B5934)*

heavy anti-tank guns and another 44 and 11 respectively under short-term repair. Thus, by the end of June, the division was perhaps at its best in spite of its losses, still relatively fresh and with the benefit of some valuable experience. It is not without reason, therefore, that 12th SS Panzer Division has been described as probably the best German division in the theatre.

The units in Meyer's division were thinly spread over a 20-km front from Fontenay-le-Pesnel east to Carpiquet and then on to the north-east of Caen. The length of this front meant that there was no defence in depth and, although there was an outpost zone, the German forward and main positions were combined around the Caen–Fontenay-le-Pesnel road. The Fontenay-le-Pesnel sector was held by 3rd Battalion of *SS-Obersturmbannführer* (Lt-Col) Wilhelm Mohnke's 26th SS Panzergrenadier Regiment (III/26th SS Panzergrenadiers), supported by the regimental reconnaissance and pioneer companies and 8th Company, 12th SS Panzer Regiment (8/12th SS Panzer Regiment), equipped with Panzer IVs. To its left, a panzergrenadier battalion of Panzer Lehr Division had taken up positions south of St-Pierre. Panzer Lehr Division was a well-equipped and respected division that had been in combat for almost three weeks by the time that Epsom began. It had a total of 63 operational Panzer IVs and Panthers and a similar number being worked on and nearly ready to return to operational status.

The Fontenay–St-Manvieu-Norrey sector was held, from left to right, by II/26th SS Panzergrenadiers, 12th SS Panzer Pioneer Battalion – elite infantry specially trained in street fighting and constructing defensive positions (north of Cheux) – and I/26th SS Panzergrenadiers as far as the Caen–Bayeux railway line. Behind them were the Panzer IVs of 6/, 5/, 7/ and 9/12th SS Panzer Regiment, each with alternative prepared positions to move to if required. Two self-propelled-gun and three towed artillery batteries were also deployed behind 26th SS Panzergrenadiers. The German gunners had worked diligently to ensure their close co-operation with the infantry in front of them. They were well aware that, together with the armour, they were likely to play a critical defensive role if the British made a concentrated attack, owing to the lack of depth in the panzergrenadiers' positions.

SS-Obersturmbannführer (Lt-Col) Karl-Heinz Milius commanded 25th SS Panzergrenadier Regiment which held the front from Franqueville to Épron north of Caen, supported by the 150-mm guns and other weapons of III/12th SS Panzer Artillery. The

Orders of Battle: Principal German Units in Operation Epsom

26 June 1944

I SS Panzer Corps ***SS-Obergruppenführer Josef 'Sepp' Dietrich***

12th SS Panzer Division 'Hitlerjugend'
SS-Standartenführer Kurt Meyer

12th SS Panzer Regiment (*SS-Panzer-Regiment 12*)	*SS-Obersturmbannführer Max Wünsche*
25th SS Panzergrenadier Regt (*SS-Panzergrenadier-Regiment 25*)	*SS-Obersturmbannführer Karl-Heinz Milius*
26th SS Panzergrenadier Regt	*SS-Obersturmbannführer Wilhelm Mohnke*
12th SS Panzer Artillery Regt (*SS-Panzerartillerie-Regiment 12*)	*SS-Obersturmbannführer Fritz Schröder*
12th SS Panzer Recce Battalion (*SS-Panzeraufklärungs-Abteilung 12*)	*SS-Sturmbannführer Gerd Bremer*
12th SS Anti-Tank Battalion (*SS-Panzerjägerabteilung 12*)	*SS-Sturmbannführer Jakob Hanreich*
12th SS Projector Battalion (*SS-Werfer-Abteilung 12*)	*SS-Sturmbannführer W. Müller*
12th SS Anti-Aircraft Battalion (*SS-Flak-Abteilung 12*)	*SS-Sturmbannführer Rudolf Fend*
12th SS Panzer Pioneer Btn (*SS-Panzerpionierbataillon 12*)	*SS-Sturmbannführer S. Müller*

II SS Panzer Corps ***SS-Obergruppenführer Willi Bittrich***

9th SS Panzer Division 'Hohenstaufen'
SS-Standartenführer Thomas Müller

9th SS Panzer Regiment	*SS-Sturmbannführer O. Meyer*
19th SS Panzergrenadier Regt	*SS-Sturmbannführer E. Zollhöfer*
20th SS Panzergrenadier Regt	*SS-Sturmbannführer R. Gruber*
9th SS Panzer Artillery Regt	*SS-Sturmbannführer L. Spindler*
9th SS Panzer Recce Btn	*SS-Hauptsturmführer V. Gräbner*
9th SS Anti-Tank Battalion	*SS-Sturmbannführer Röstel*
9th SS Anti-Aircraft Btn	*SS-Sturmbannführer Dr Loeniker*
9th SS Panzer Pioneer Btn	*SS-Sturmbannführer P. Monich*

10th SS Panzer Division 'Frundsberg'
SS-Oberführer Heinz Harmel

10th SS-Panzer Regiment	*SS-Obersturmbannführer O. Paetsch*
21st SS Panzergrenadier Regt	*SS-Standartenführer E. Diesenhofer*
22nd SS Panzergrenadier Regt	*SS-Sturmbannführer Schulze*
10th SS Panzer Artillery Regt	*SS-Sturmbannführer H. Sander*
10th SS Panzer Recce Btn	*SS-Sturmbannführer H. Brinkmann*
10th SS Anti-Aircraft Btn	*SS-Hauptsturmführer Schrembs*
10th SS Panzer Pioneer Btn	*SS-Sturmbannführer Tröbinger*

divisional reserve, positioned to the north of Noyers-Bocage, was 12th SS Panzer Reconnaissance Battalion and I/12th SS Panzers, equipped with Panthers. This was not a particularly strong reserve and so, as Epsom approached, I SS Panzer Corps moved two companies of Tiger tanks of 101st Heavy SS Panzer Battalion – a corps asset – into the area behind 26th SS Panzergrenadier Regiment. Behind 12th SS Panzer Division and Panzer Lehr Division were elements of III Anti-Aircraft Corps, comprising four regiments each consisting of 30–40 88-mm guns and a number of lighter pieces, with 4th Anti-Aircraft Regiment of this corps in the area Mouen–Noyers-Bocage–Évrecy.

These were the divisions already *in situ* at the front, but as it became clear to the Germans that the Normandy invasion might be the Allies' main effort and not a feint, six other armoured divisions began to move to the area in order to launch a counter-attack. Of those that were to play a part in the coming battle on the Odon, 2nd SS Panzer Division *Das Reich* was moving up from the south of France and *SS-Obergruppenführer* (Lt-Gen) Paul Hausser's II SS Panzer Corps, consisting of 9th SS Panzer Division *Hohenstaufen* and 10th SS Panzer Division *Frundsberg*, came from Russia. The counter-attack, as already mentioned, was to be focused on Bayeux as a means of dividing the British and American armies before destroying them piecemeal. A great Allied strength, however, severely disrupted these divisions before they even reached Normandy. Air power, so critical at every level of the war, slowed the assembly of these forces by bombing raids throughout France and the Low Countries (assisted by Allied special forces and the Resistance) targeting the transport network as well as the actual divisions themselves. II SS Panzer Corps was, therefore, forced off the railway network and had to complete most of its journey through France by road. Thus, the divisions assembling in Normandy for the major counter-attack arrived in dribs and drabs, late, tired and having been reduced in their combat effectiveness.

VIII Corps

As the Germans sought to ensure that their front to the west of Caen was as strong as possible in order to receive another major attack on Caen and worked on their plans for a counter-attack, Montgomery worried in the wake of the Great Storm as to whether his preparation for Operation Epsom had been completely ruined. Lt-Gen Sir Richard O'Connor's VIII Corps included 15th (Scottish)

Rifleman R. Oates and Sergeant James Woodward take up a position with a Projector Infantry Anti-Tank (PIAT) in a cornfield somewhere on the Epsom battlefield. *(IWM B6185)*

Division, commanded by Major-General (Maj-Gen) G.H.A. MacMillan; 11th Armoured Division commanded by 37-year-old Maj-Gen G.P.B. 'Pip' Roberts and 43rd (Wessex) Division commanded by Maj-Gen G.I. Thomas. It also included two independent tank brigades, 31st Tank Brigade and 4th Armoured Brigade (the only experienced formation in the corps, having fought in the Western Desert). VIII Corps therefore totalled some 60,000 men and over 600 tanks. In support were some 736 guns including those of XXX Corps and I Corps on the flanks, the heavy and medium artillery regiments of 8th Army Group Royal Artillery (AGRA) and naval gunfire support from three cruisers and the monitor, HMS *Roberts*. Close air support was to be provided by the RAF's Second Tactical Air Force and the preliminary bombing of the battlefield was to be carried out by 250 RAF heavy bombers.

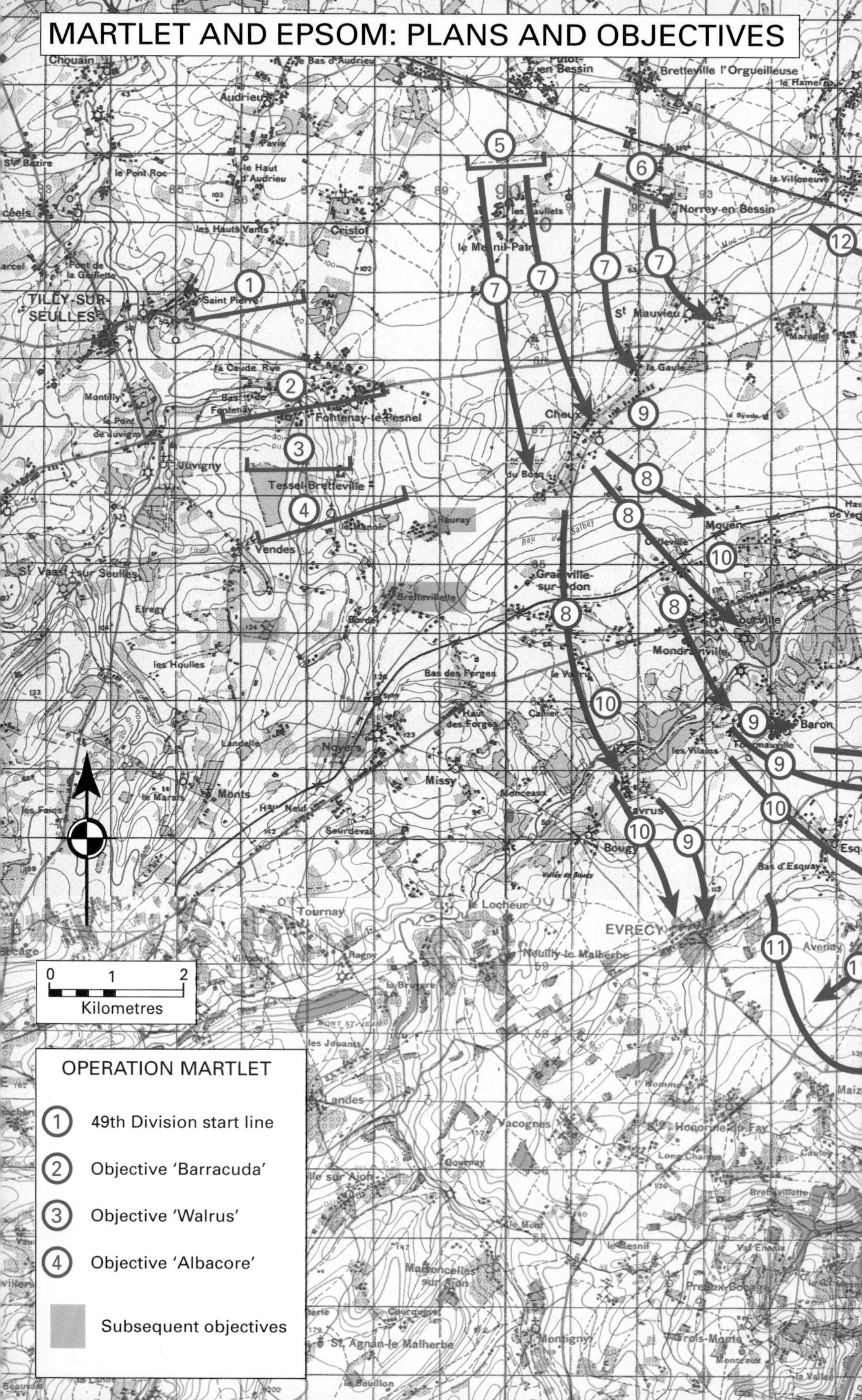

MARTLET AND EPSOM: PLANS AND OBJECTIVES
OPERATION MARTLET
1 49th Division start line
2 Objective 'Barracuda'
3 Objective 'Walrus'
4 Objective 'Albacore'
Subsequent objectives
Kilometres
TILLY-SUR-SEULLES
Fontenay-le-Pesnel
Tessel-Bretteville
Vendes
Cheux
St Mauvieu
Norrey-en-Bessin
Bretteville l'Orgueilleuse
Grainville-sur-Odon
Mondrainville
Baron
Noyers
Missy
EVRECY

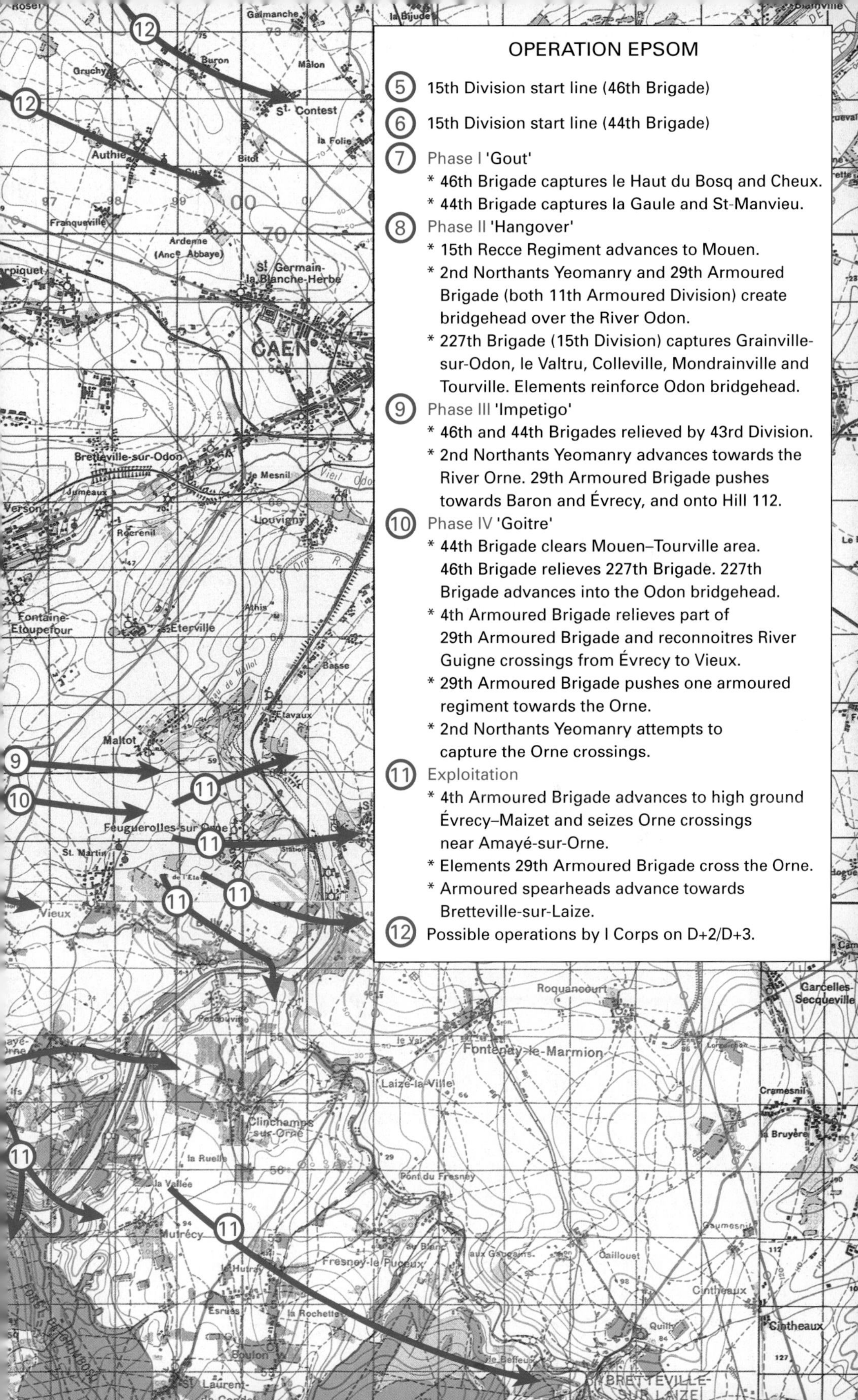
OPERATION EPSOM
5 15th Division start line (46th Brigade)
6 15th Division start line (44th Brigade)
7 Phase I 'Gout'
* 46th Brigade captures le Haut du Bosq and Cheux.
* 44th Brigade captures la Gaule and St-Manvieu.
8 Phase II 'Hangover'
* 15th Recce Regiment advances to Mouen.
* 2nd Northants Yeomanry and 29th Armoured Brigade (both 11th Armoured Division) create bridgehead over the River Odon.
* 227th Brigade (15th Division) captures Grainville-sur-Odon, le Valtru, Colleville, Mondrainville and Tourville. Elements reinforce Odon bridgehead.
9 Phase III 'Impetigo'
* 46th and 44th Brigades relieved by 43rd Division.
* 2nd Northants Yeomanry advances towards the River Orne. 29th Armoured Brigade pushes towards Baron and Évrecy, and onto Hill 112.
10 Phase IV 'Goitre'
* 44th Brigade clears Mouen–Tourville area. 46th Brigade relieves 227th Brigade. 227th Brigade advances into the Odon bridgehead.
* 4th Armoured Brigade relieves part of 29th Armoured Brigade and reconnoitres River Guigne crossings from Évrecy to Vieux.
* 29th Armoured Brigade pushes one armoured regiment towards the Orne.
* 2nd Northants Yeomanry attempts to capture the Orne crossings.
11 Exploitation
* 4th Armoured Brigade advances to high ground Évrecy–Maizet and seizes Orne crossings near Amayé-sur-Orne.
* Elements 29th Armoured Brigade cross the Orne.
* Armoured spearheads advance towards Bretteville-sur-Laize.
12 Possible operations by I Corps on D+2/D+3.
Galmanche
Buron
Mâlon
Gruchy
St. Contest
la Folie
Authie
Bitot
Franqueville
Ardenne
(Ancᵉ Abbaye)
St. Germain-la-Blanche-Herbe
CAEN
Bretteville-sur-Odon
le Mesnil
Jumeaux
Verson
Rocreuil
Louvigny
Fontaine-Etoupefour
Eterville
Athis
Basse
Etavaux
Maltot
Feuguerolles-sur-Orne
St. Martin
Vieux
Roquancourt
Garcelles-Secqueville
Fontenay-le-Marmion
le Val
Laize-la-Ville
Cramesnil
Clinchamps-sur-Orne
la Bruyère
la Ruelle
Pont du Fresney
la Vallée
Mutrécy
Caillouet
Fresney-le-Puceaux
Cintheaux
la Rochette
Esrues
Boulon
Quilly
St. Laurent-de-Condel
BRETTEVILLE-SUR-LAIZE

The Plan

Epsom and the supporting operations were worked on by staffs in their various headquarters. Maj-Gen E.H. 'Bubbles' Barker and his 49th Division staff worked on Martlet, the clearing of the high ground of the Rauray spur. The plan for the division, consisting of 146th, 147th and 70th Brigades, supported by 8th Armoured Brigade, was to attack at the junction between 12th SS Panzer Division and Panzer Lehr Division between Tilly-sur-Seulles and Boislonde. The division was then to launch a phased advance: 146th and 147th Brigades, with armoured support, were to open the assault by seizing Fontenay-le-Pesnel and then 146th Brigade was to attack across the Caen–Caumont road to take the northern end of Tessel Wood. It would then advance to protect the right flank of 147th Brigade, which was to take the Rauray spur.

Lt Welsh briefs No. 18 Platoon, 9th Cameronians, on 25 June. (IWM B5983)

VIII Corps was to launch Operation Epsom on the following morning and was to benefit from the denial of the high ground on its right flank to the Germans by 49th Division. O'Connor was also to advance in steps: 15th Division would clear up to the River Odon, starting at 0730 hours after the heavy bomber raid and a short preliminary bombardment. On a 5,000-metre front, 44th Brigade and 46th Brigade, supported by 31st Tank Brigade, were to advance and take four villages beyond the River Mue. Then,

11th Armoured Division's 29th Armoured Brigade would seize the river crossings and create a bridgehead supported by the division's 159th Brigade.

Meanwhile, 15th Division's 227th Brigade was to seize the line of the Caen–Villers-Bocage road, clear the Odon valley and then take over the defence of the bridges. At this point 29th Armoured Brigade, supported by 227th Brigade if necessary, was to cross Hill 112 to the south of the Odon and drive for the River Orne, to be replaced by 44th and 46th Brigades of 15th Division, which themselves were to be relieved to the north of the Odon by 43rd (Wessex) Division. In the final phase 4th Armoured Brigade was to cross the Orne, establish a bridgehead with 11th Armoured Division's 159th Brigade and take the high ground at Bretteville-sur-Laize.

Men of 9th Cameronians attend a service led by Reverend S. Cook just behind the front line during the afternoon of 25 June. These men were to go into battle for the first time on the following day. *(IWM B5980)*

This plan was ambitious and, whilst the reasons for its conception are understandable, even if Montgomery's actual motivations are

VIII CORPS *Lt-Gen Sir Richard O'Connor*

VIII Corps Troops
91st Anti-Tank Regiment, RA; 121st Anti-Aircraft Regiment, RA
21st Army Group Troops *(under command VIII Corps for Epsom)*
8th Army Group Royal Artillery
79th Armoured Division Troops
141st Regiment, RAC

11th Armoured Division *Maj-Gen G.P.B. Roberts*

29th Armoured Brigade *Brig C.B.C. Harvey*
23rd Hussars
3rd Battalion, The Royal Tank Regiment
2nd Fife and Forfar Yeomanry
8th Battalion, The Rifle Brigade (Motor)
13th (Honourable Artillery Company) Regiment, Royal Horse Artillery
119th Battery, 75th Anti-Tank Regiment, RA

159th Infantry Brigade *Brig J.G. Sandie*
4th Battalion, The King's Shropshire Light Infantry
1st Battalion, The Herefordshire Regiment
3rd Battalion, The Monmouthshire Regiment
2nd (Independent) Machine-Gun Coy, Royal Northumberland Fusiliers
151st (Ayrshire Yeomanry) Field Regt, RA; 117th Anti-Tank Bty, RA;
81st Squadron, 6th Assault Regiment, RE

Divisional Troops
2nd Northamptonshire Yeomanry (less A Squadron);
77th Medium Regiment, RA; 75th Anti-Tank Regiment, RA;
58th Light AA Regiment, RA (part); Counter-Mortar Battery, RA;
13th, 612th, 147th Field Park Squadrons, RE; 10th Bridging Troop, RE

15th (Scottish) Infantry Division *Maj-Gen G.H. MacMillan*

44th (Lowland) Infantry Brigade *Brig H.D.K. Money*
8th Battalion, The Royal Scots (The Royal Regiment)
6th Battalion, The Royal Scots Fusiliers
6th Battalion, The King's Own Scottish Borderers
141st (The Buffs) Regiment, RAC
A Company, 1st Battalion, The Middlesex Regiment (Machine Gun)
190th Field Regiment, RA; 159th Anti-Tank Bty, RA; Light AA Bty, RA;
81st Squadron, 6th Assault Regiment, RE; 279th Field Company, RE

46th (Highland) Infantry Brigade *Brig C.M. Barber*
9th Battalion, The Cameronians (Scottish Rifles)
2nd Battalion, The Glasgow Highlanders
7th Battalion, The Seaforth Highlanders
A Squadron, 2nd Northamptonshire Yeomanry *(under command)*
141st (The Buffs) Regiment, RAC (two troops Crocodiles)
B Company, 1st Battalion, The Middlesex Regiment (Machine Gun)
181st Field Regiment, RA; 161st Anti-Tank Bty, RA; Light AA Bty, RA;
81st Squadron, 6th Assault Regiment, RE; 278th Field Company, RE

227th (Highland) Infantry Brigade *Brig J.R. Mackintosh-Walker*

10th Battalion, The Highland Light Infantry (City of Glasgow Regiment)
2nd Battalion, The Gordon Highlanders
2nd Battalion, The Argyll and Sutherland Highlanders
C Company, 1st Battalion, The Middlesex Regiment (Machine Gun)
131st Field Regiment, RA; 286th Anti-Tank Battery, RA;
391st Light AA Battery, RA; 20th Field Company, RE

Divisional Troops

15th Reconnaissance Regiment, RAC; HQ and 346th Battery,
97th Anti-Tank Regt, RA; HQ, 119th Light AA Regt, RA;
HQ, 15th Division Engineers Regt; 624th Field Park Coy, RE;
26th Bridging Platoon, RE

43rd (Wessex) Infantry Division *Maj-Gen G.I. Thomas*

129th Infantry Brigade *Brig G.H.L. Luce*

4th Battalion, The Somerset Light Infantry
4th Battalion, The Wiltshire Regiment
5th Battalion, The Wiltshire Regiment
A Company, 8th Battalion, The Middlesex Regiment (Machine Gun)
94th (Dorset and Hampshire) Field Regt, RA; 235th Anti-Tank Bty, RA;
Support Troop, 360th Light AA Bty, RA;
30th Independent AA Troop, RA; 206th Field Company, RE

130th Infantry Brigade *Brig N.D. Leslie*

7th Battalion, The Hampshire Regiment
4th Battalion, The Dorsetshire Regiment
5th Battalion, The Dorsetshire Regiment
B Company, 8th Battalion, The Middlesex Regiment (Machine Gun)
112th (Wessex) Field Regiment, RA; 223rd Anti-Tank Battery, RA;
Support Troop, 362nd Light AA Battery, RA;
32nd Independent AA Troop, RA; 553rd Field Company, RE

214th Infantry Brigade *Brig H. Essame*

7th Battalion, The Somerset Light Infantry
1st Battalion, The Worcestershire Regiment
5th Battalion, The Duke of Cornwall's Light Infantry
C Company, 8th Battalion, The Middlesex Regiment (Machine Gun)
179th Field Regiment, RA; 333rd Anti-Tank Battery, RA;
Support Troop, 361st Light AA Battery, RA;
31st Independent AA Troop, RA; 204th Field Company, RE

Divisional Troops

43rd (Gloucestershire) Reconnaissance Regiment, RAC
HQ, 8th Battalion, The Middlesex Regiment (Machine Gun)
HQ and 236th Battery, 59th (Hampshire) Anti-Tank Regiment, RA;
HQ, 360th and 362nd Batteries, 110th (7th Dorset) Light AA Regt, RA;
HQ, 43rd Division Engineers Regiment; 207th Field Park Coy, RE

Supporting Armour

31st Independent Tank Brigade contained 3,400 officers, NCOs and men. It comprised three tank battalions, each consisting of 52 Churchills, 11 Stuarts, 2 Churchill 'forward observation' tanks, 6 anti-aircraft tanks and 6 Churchill 95-mm howitzers with attached REME, and a headquarters squadron consisting of 4 Churchills, 3 Churchill bridge-layers, 2 anti-aircraft tanks and 10 scout cars. It also had the following attached units: brigade signals (Royal Corps of Signals); a central workshop (Royal Electrical and Mechanical Engineers); a Royal Army Service Corps company; a light field ambulance (Royal Army Medical Corps); a mobile field park (Royal Army Ordnance Corps) and a delivery squadron (Royal Armoured Corps).

31st Tank Brigade *Brig G.S. Knight*
(under command of 15th Division for Epsom)
7th Battalion, The Royal Tank Regiment
9th Battalion, The Royal Tank Regiment
C Squadron, 2nd County of London Yeomanry (Westminster Dragoons)
B Squadron, 22nd Dragoons

4th Armoured Brigade had a similar organisation to 31st Tank Brigade, but used Sherman tanks not Churchills. The Sherman was faster than the Churchill, and therefore better suited to the exploitation role. Unlike tank brigades, armoured brigades possessed a motorised infantry battalion and artillery elements to help them consolidate objectives when operating independently.

4th Armoured Brigade *Brig J.C.C. Currie*
(under command of 11th Armoured Division for Epsom)
The Royal Scots Greys (2nd Dragoons)
3rd County of London Yeomanry (The Sharpshooters)
44th Battalion, The Royal Tank Regiment
2nd Battalion, The King's Royal Rifle Corps (Motor)
4th Regiment, Royal Horse Artillery
144th Anti-Tank Battery, RA (Self-Propelled)

still a moot point, it would take considerable good fortune to make it work. The terrain, as discussed above, was immensely favourable to the defender, but there were further obstacles to British success. The front was narrow (just over 5 km) and yet the plan required that huge numbers of men and quantities of armour be poured through it, necessitating secure flanks and the attainment of considerable momentum if the attack was not going to suffocate itself. However, the likelihood of that momentum being attained was greatly reduced by the terrain and the strongly fortified villages that studded it. Moreover, streams, rivers and a railway line all cut across the battlefield, providing yet more obstacles to overcome, while only two minor roads led southwards from Cheux in the central northern part of the battlefield. In such circumstances, fair

A Churchill tank of 31st Tank Brigade. As infantry support armour they played a critical role in Operation Epsom, but were often impeded by the particularly difficult terrain found on the Epsom battlefield. *(IWM B6002)*

flying weather for close air support was essential as were relevant fighting methods based on all-arms co-operation. The weather forecast, however, was poor and VIII Corps consisted largely of untried troops.

23–25 June 1944: Preliminary Operations

Second (British) Army opened its new offensive phase with 51st Division's attack out of the Orne bridgehead before dawn on 23 June. In this, 152nd Brigade seized Ste-Honorine la Chardronette in a surprise attack and then spent the rest of the day rebuffing counter-attacks by Battlegroup *von Luck*, which was based on units of 21st Panzer Division to the east of the Orne. The attack was not only a success in that it took an important village, it also put pressure on the Germans to ready themselves for further attacks in this area, thus diverting attention and resources away from the growing force and preparations on the opposite side of Caen.

In the days immediately before 26 June, units of VIII Corps readied themselves and, during the night of 24/25 June, moved

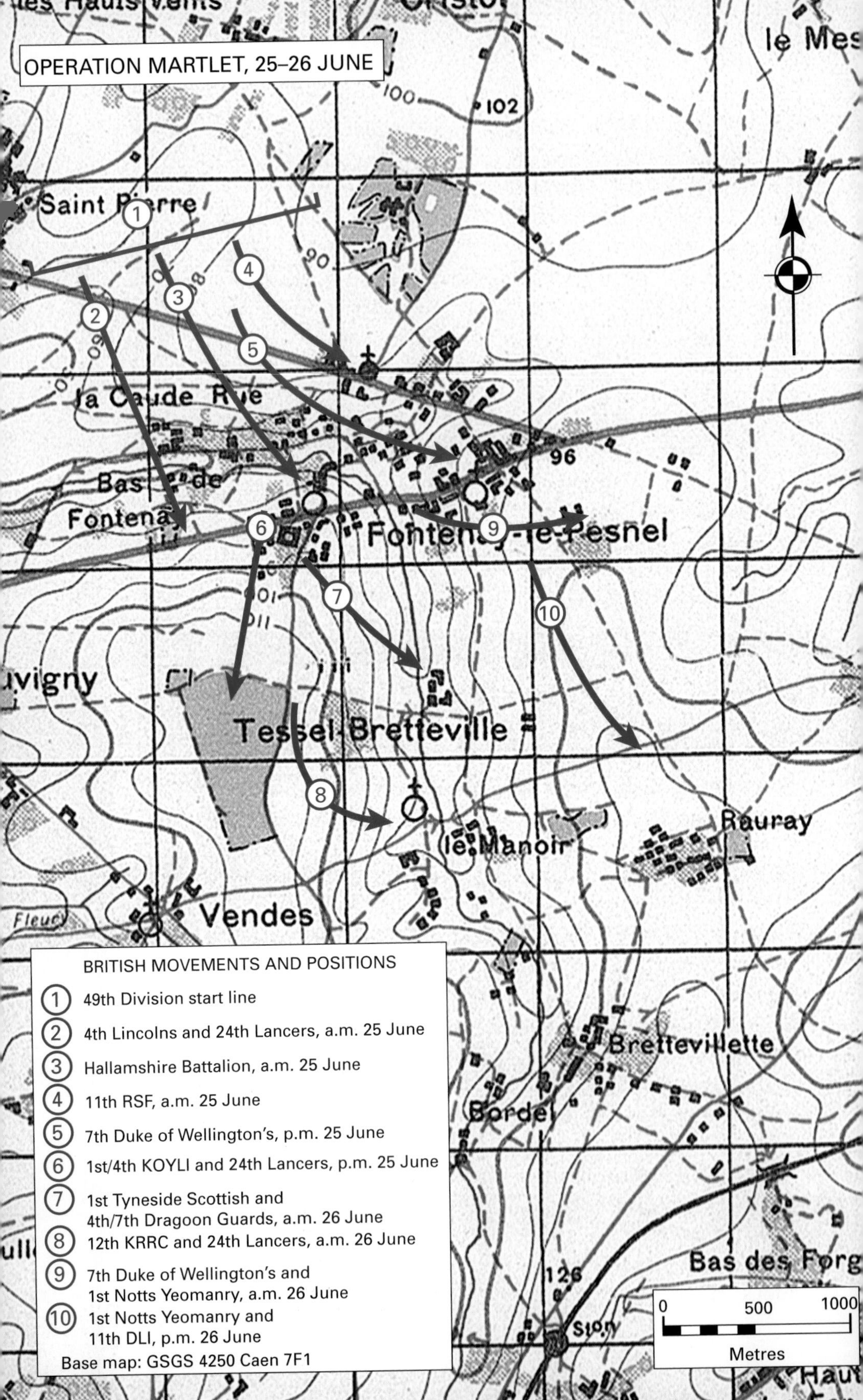
OPERATION MARTLET, 25–26 JUNE
Saint Pierre
la Caude Rue
Bas de Fontenay
Fontenay-le-Pesnel
Tessel-Bretteville
le Manoir
Rauray
Vendes
Brettevillette
Bordel
Bas des Forg
le Mes
102
100
96
126
BRITISH MOVEMENTS AND POSITIONS
1 49th Division start line
2 4th Lincolns and 24th Lancers, a.m. 25 June
3 Hallamshire Battalion, a.m. 25 June
4 11th RSF, a.m. 25 June
5 7th Duke of Wellington's, p.m. 25 June
6 1st/4th KOYLI and 24th Lancers, p.m. 25 June
7 1st Tyneside Scottish and 4th/7th Dragoon Guards, a.m. 26 June
8 12th KRRC and 24th Lancers, a.m. 26 June
9 7th Duke of Wellington's and 1st Notts Yeomanry, a.m. 26 June
10 1st Notts Yeomanry and 11th DLI, p.m. 26 June
Base map: GSGS 4250 Caen 7F1
0
500
1000
Metres

forward to their assembly areas. That morning, these troops, the vast majority of whom had never been in action before, were drawn at 0415 hours to the noise of battle to the south-west. There, the novice 49th Division had launched Operation Martlet, supported by 8th Armoured Brigade and 250 guns.

There were three objectives for the attack: 'Barracuda' was the road between Juvigny-sur-Seulles and Fontenay-le-Pesnel; 'Walrus' was from the northern end of Tessel Wood to the farm at St-Nicolas; and 'Albacore' was the Rauray spur and Point 110. Three infantry battalions struck out for Barracuda, 4th Lincolns on the right, the Hallamshire Battalion in the centre and 11th Royal Scots on the left. 1st Tyneside Scots was in reserve. On the right 4th Lincolns, with the Shermans of 24th Lancers in support, attacked through the mist and eventually reached the Barracuda line and dug in. In the centre the Hallamshire Battalion found its way forward to the Juvigny–Fontenay road, but was then hit by heavy tank and machine-gun fire from 8/12th SS Panzers and two companies of III/26th SS Panzergrenadiers. On the left 11th Royal Scots fought to get to the north side of Fontenay-le-Pesnel and tried to break into the village all day. 7th Duke of Wellington's eventually moved up to relieve 11th Royal Scots, but only managed to clear some of the western parts of Fontenay-le-Pesnel.

Meanwhile, the next phase, Walrus, had begun. On the right 4th King's Own Yorkshire Light Infantry advanced through 4th Lincolns on the Fontenay-le-Pesnel road and took Tessel Wood, supported by 24th Lancers. A series of German counter-attacks followed, conducted by III/26th SS Panzergrenadiers supported by 8/12th SS Panzers, but these were frustrated by British artillery and air power and failed. As a result of the British advance in this area, at 1400 hours three Panther companies from I/12th SS Panzers, supported by III/26th SS Panzergrenadiers and 12th SS Panzer Reconnaissance Battalion, were sent to plug the gap that had developed and link up with Panzer Lehr Division on their left. On 49th Division's left, meanwhile, 147th Brigade should have been attacking south of Fontenay-le-Pesnel but was still trying to clear the village, having run into III/26th SS Panzergrenadiers, supported by elements of the regimental reconnaissance, pioneer and infantry-gun companies, and Panzer IV tanks of II/12th SS Panzers.

By the end of the day, 49th Division had achieved a great deal but was still some way short of the Rauray spur. Nevertheless, the attack had wrong-footed the Germans.

During the evening of 25 June a German Seventh Army report stated:

'After heavy fighting on the severely weakened left of 12th SS Panzer Division and right of Panzer Lehr Division, attacks by successive waves of enemy troops, supported in the air by continuous enemy sorties, succeeded in tearing open a gap 5 km wide and 2 km deep.'

Source: Seventh Army War Diary, 25 June 1944, RG 407, Box 24154, File 488, US National Archives.

A 17-pounder anti-tank gun moving forward on 25 June. *(IWM B5992)*

The German response during the night was to withdraw from Fontenay-le-Pesnel in order to straighten their line, a move which allowed the village to be taken by the British at dawn on 26 June. However, the chances of seizing the critical high ground of the Rauray spur before Epsom was launched just a few hours later were slim. Even so, 49th Division put in another attack that morning – just as the Germans were launching their own counter-attack. Ordered by Dietrich to use 12th SS Panzer Division and Panzer

Lehr Division to restore the original line, Meyer complained unavailingly that he did not have the forces for such a task and was ordered to concentrate armour from 12th SS Panzer Regiment to support III/26th SS Panzergrenadiers against 49th Division. Unknown to Dietrich, this left just three battalions (that is the remainder of 26th SS Panzergrenadier Regiment and 12th SS Panzer Pioneer Battalion) to defend against the coming VIII Corps attack.

25 June: after the attack on Fontenay-le-Pesnel, cattle lie dead on the battlefield. Troops on both sides sometimes found that their positions were given away by inquisitive cattle wandering over to see what was going on. *(IWM B5938)*

Operation Epsom D-1

Meanwhile, as 49th Division struggled forward on 25 June, VIII Corps made the final preparations for its own attack the following morning. With the majority of the guns having moved forward already and been concealed in barns, orchards and woods, the infantry moved up to areas just behind the front line. Some of the units had only just arrived in Normandy because of the storms and there was precious little time for them to adjust to the conditions and engage in detailed reconnaissance before the officers received their orders. Indeed, when reconnaissance teams did find their way to the ruined villages near the front line, they found at le Mesnil-Patry, for example, that narrow sunken lanes were an obstacle both to their tanks and a cohesive infantry advance. Moreover, at Norrey-en-Bessin their left flank was swept by German fire from Carpiquet airfield; the village of St-Manvieu-Norrey could not be seen as it was in a fold in the ground; and much of the terrain to its south was hidden from sight by Ring Contour 100 (about 1 km south of Cheux in the area marked as le Gros Orme on modern maps). Nevertheless, during the night of 25/26 June, the infantry and supporting armour of 15th Division moved up to the front line to positions that ran from a point just north of le Mesnil-Patry eastward to Norrey-en-Bessin.

> **That evening Montgomery signalled to General Eisenhower, the Supreme Allied Commander:**
>
> 'Blitz attack of 8 Corps goes in tomorrow at 0730 hrs and once it starts I will continue the battle on the eastern flank till one of us cracks and it will NOT be us.'
>
> *Source:* Nigel Hamilton, *Monty: Master of the Battlefield*, page 691.

CHAPTER 2

26 JUNE

OPERATION MARTLET

The 49th Division attack began at 0650 hours, two hours after dawn, in an attempt to make progress towards the Rauray ridge, but as importantly to put pressure on the Germans just as Epsom was beginning. In the centre of the battlefield, an attack by 1st Tyneside Scots of 70th Brigade and the tanks of 4th/7th Royal Dragoon Guards sought to capture la Grande Ferme on the River Bordel before crossing the stream and seizing Rauray. On their right 12th King's Royal Rifle Corps (KRRC) and 24th Lancers were to advance from Tessel Wood towards Brettevillette. Due to the requirements of the Epsom offensive, however, there was little artillery support. The 1st Tyneside Scots' attack immediately ran into *Nebelwerfer* fire, German riflemen and machine guns that slowed everything down. The battalion struggled to the Bordel stream, crossed it and then, at around noon, ran into four well dug-in tanks of I/12th SS Panzers and infantry from II/26th SS Panzergrenadiers and 21st Panzer Division's 192nd Panzergrenadier Regiment. These moves coincided exactly with 12th SS Panzer

Division's counter-attack to restore its former front line and an intense tank battle developed.

Kurt Meyer watched the clash from Rauray:

'A bitterly contested tank versus tank action develops. The hedgerows, difficult to see through, don't allow our tanks to take advantage of their guns' longer range. Lack of infantry is an especial disadvantage. Intense artillery fire makes co-operation enormously difficult and effective command and control virtually impossible... '

Source: quoted in Michael Reynolds, *Steel Inferno*, p. 123.

A Royal Artillery 5.5-inch gun firing in support of 15th Division's attack on 26 June. *(IWM B5936)*

49th Division made little if any progress and was under intense pressure in many areas when Meyer was told that a major attack had commenced to the east. Meyer immediately stopped his counter-attack and adopted a defensive posture on the Rauray spur, ordering the Panzer IV companies to return as quickly as possible to their positions behind 26th SS Panzergrenadier Regiment. Meyer then headed back to his divisional headquarters in Verson. At around

1600 hours 1st Tyneside Scots was withdrawn. German observers, however, continued to overlook the Epsom battlefield from the Rauray ridge.

XXX CORPS ***Lt-Gen G.C. Bucknall***

49th (West Riding) Infantry Division ***Maj-Gen E.H. Barker***

70th Infantry Brigade *Brig E.C. Cooke-Collis*

1st Battalion, The Tyneside Scottish
10th Battalion, The Durham Light Infantry
11th Battalion, The Durham Light Infantry
C Company, 2nd Battalion, The Kensington Regiment (Machine Gun)
185th Field Regiment, RA; 217th Anti-Tank Battery, RA;
Support Troop, Light Anti-Aircraft Battery, RA; 757th Field Company, RE

146th Infantry Brigade *Brig J.F. Walker*

4th Battalion, The Lincolnshire Regiment
4th Battalion, The King's Own Yorkshire Light Infantry
Hallamshire Battalion, The York and Lancaster Regiment
A Company, 2nd Battalion, The Kensington Regiment (Machine Gun)
69th Field Regiment, RA; 218th Anti-Tank Battery, RA;
Support Troop, Light Anti-Aircraft Battery, RA; 294th Field Company, RE

147th Infantry Brigade *Brig E.R. Mahony*

11th Battalion, The Royal Scots (The Royal Regiment)
6th Battalion, The Duke of Wellington's Regiment (West Riding)
7th Battalion, The Duke of Wellington's Regiment (West Riding)
B Company, 2nd Battalion, The Kensington Regiment (Machine Gun)
143rd Field Regiment, RA; 219th Anti-Tank Battery, RA;
Support Troop, Light Anti-Aircraft Battery, RA; 756th Field Company, RE

Divisional Troops

49th Reconnaissance Regiment, RAC
HQ, 2nd Battalion, The Kensington Regiment (Machine Gun)
HQ and 220th Battery, 55th (Suffolk Yeomanry) Anti-Tank Regt, RA;
HQ, 89th Light Anti-Aircraft Regiment, RA;
HQ, 49th Division Engineers Regiment; 289th Field Park Company, RE

8th Armoured Brigade *Brig H.J.B. Cracroft*

24th Lancers
4th/7th Royal Dragoon Guards
1st Nottinghamshire (Sherwood Rangers) Yeomanry
12th Battalion, The King's Royal Rifle Corps (Motor)
147th (Essex Yeomanry) Field Regiment, RA (Self Propelled);
Anti-Tank Battery, RA

On the right/west of 1st Tyneside Scots, 12th KRRC attacked south to Tessel with 24th Lancers alongside Tessel Wood. They fought their way to the crossroads between Vendes and Tessel, and then struggled to the western edge of Tessel itself but, too weak to hold their position, they then withdrew back to Tessel Wood. On the left flank that morning, 7th Duke of Wellington's of 147th Brigade, supported by the armour of 1st Nottinghamshire Yeomanry, attacked out of Fontenay-le-Pesnel towards St-Nicolas farm, which was defended by 6/26th SS Panzergrenadiers and some tanks. The initial attack failed, but in mid-afternoon, after a very heavy 20-minute bombardment, a renewed effort was successful. This thrust was so effective that the armour pushed on 1.5 km past the farm and stopped just short of Rauray, eventually being joined that evening by 70th Brigade's 11th Durham Light Infantry (DLI). In fact Rauray was not taken on 26 June, but there was considerable optimism that it would finally fall to the British attack on the following day, and it should not be forgotten that in any case the attack was a distraction to the Germans as they reacted to Epsom.

Operation Epsom

Operation Epsom began in unseasonal rain and mist that dampened the spirits of the troops across Normandy, but caused wider concern in VIII Corps because the battlefield was turning into a quagmire. Moreover, the weather conditions forced the cancellation of the planned bombing raid and any close air support. The troops, meanwhile, did not hear the reassuring sound of the aerial battlefield preparation that they had expected. The first major blast that they heard came from the British artillery, which opened up at 0720 hours on the outpost zone of 12th SS Panzer Division. Ten minutes later the infantry and tanks advanced as the barrage rolled across the German positions. 15th Division's 44th Brigade and 46th Brigade were supported by 9th Royal Tank Regiment (RTR) and 7th RTR respectively and a number of 79th Armoured Division's specialised assault vehicles, the 'funnies'. 44th Brigade was to take St-Manvieu-Norrey and la Gaule, whilst 46th Brigade was to take Cheux and le Haut du Bosq before 29th Armoured Brigade and 227th Brigade took the fighting on to the Odon.

> **Kurt Meyer later wrote:**
>
> 'This is the major attack I expected! The cornerstone of the German front in Normandy is now at stake. Caen, the target, is to be smothered by an enveloping attack. Caen is to be Montgomery's prize, bringing about the collapse of the German front.'
>
> *Source:* Kurt Meyer, *Grenadiers*, p. 136.

A Churchill tank advances through a cornfield on the morning of 26 June, followed by the infantry. *(IWM B5956)*

The Germans stoically allowed the creeping barrage and the first waves of infantry to pass over their skilfully camouflaged positions and then opened fire, causing great confusion. Meanwhile, from the Rauray spur, observers directed the guns of tanks and the artillery on to the advancing British troops with great success. On 44th Brigade's left, 6th Royal Scots Fusiliers (RSF) and B Squadron, 9th RTR, advanced behind the British barrage and into the killing ground. 6th RSF suffered some casualties and, in common with the

other attacking battalions, the exploding shells, smoke, mist, and isolated German riflemen all caused considerable disorientation. Nevertheless, 6th RSF reached the village of St-Manvieu-Norrey at 0830 hours and then, after another couple of hours of fighting, broke in. By about noon the defenders of I/26th SS Panzergrenadiers had been overrun except for those in a few strongpoints. The vicious hand-to-hand fighting in and around these was typical of these highly-trained and motivated young *Waffen-SS* soldiers and lasted for the rest of the day before the village was securely in British hands.

Meanwhile, on the right, 8th Royal Scots and A Squadron, 9th RTR, advanced on la Gaule. They suffered similar problems to those encountered by 6th RSF and were slowed down so that they no longer followed close behind their barrage. Even so the battalion reached the Caen–Fontenay-le-Pesnel road (now the D9) at 0930 hours; an hour later it reached la Gaule, which it cleared quickly and then successfully consolidated. The success in la Gaule was probably in no small part due to the fact that 8th Royal Scots attacked on the boundary between I/26th SS Panzergrenadiers and 12th SS Panzer Pioneer Battalion.

On 46th Brigade's front the village objectives were considerably further away. On the left, 2nd Glasgow Highlanders, supported by B Squadron, 7th RTR, headed towards Cheux. On the right, 9th Cameronians, supported by C Squadron, 7th RTR, moved to le Haut du Bosq. These two battalions also advanced through the mist and rain and within a short time came across an anti-tank minefield. This skilfully placed obstacle held the armour up – 7th RTR alone lost nine tanks – and while it was cleared the infantry carried on, unsupported, into a hail of fire. As the barrage rolled on, the infantry soon lost contact with it, which made them even more vulnerable to the carefully sited German defences. Nevertheless, as the British infantry slowed down, the armour caught them up again and the thrust continued. The battle for the critical road junction of Cheux was intense, bloody and protracted. 2nd Glasgow Highlanders assaulted the village at around 1030 hours and found stubborn German resistance. The fighting continued throughout the day and both sides suffered heavy casualties. On the right, 9th Cameronians pushed through to le Haut du Bosq but was hit hard on its final approach at about 1100 hours by 12th SS Panzer Artillery Regiment and fire from the Rauray spur. Crocodile flamethrowers were called forward to deal with the German strongpoints and the infantry entered the village at around 1130 hours. 9th Cameronians secured the northern part of the village, but the southern area and the woods on either side remained in German hands as the Panzer IVs of 5/12th SS Panzers and 8/12th SS Panzers, returning from the fight at Rauray, stopped the advance of 7th RTR around the village.

Men of 6th Royal Scots Fusiliers entering St-Manvieu-Norrey on the morning of 26 June. *(IWM B5961)*

Operation Epsom Artillery

11th Armoured Division	48 x 25-pounder
15th (Scottish) Division	96 x 25-pounder
43rd (Wessex) Division	72 x 25-pounder
4th Armoured Brigade	24 x 25-pounder
8th AGRA	16 x heavy guns
	16 x 5.5-inch & 4.5-inch
	24 x 3.7-inch anti-aircraft guns
Total	**296 guns**
Available from flanking corps:	
I Corps	216 field guns
	32 medium guns
	16 heavy guns
XXX Corps	96 field guns
	64 medium guns
	16 heavy guns
	24 x 3.7-inch anti-aircraft guns
Total	**440 guns**
GRAND TOTAL	**736 guns**

Meanwhile, as the villages were being cleared, 7th Seaforths, 46th Brigade's reserve battalion, moved forward in preparation for an attack from Cheux to take the important high ground just beyond known as Ring Contour 100. As the men of 7th Seaforths advanced they were badly hit by artillery fire and the still-hidden German riflemen. Moving to the crest of the position, the attack suffered heavy casualties in men and among the supporting tanks and the battalion was forced to withdraw a little and to dig in on the northern slope.

The first attacks in Epsom had been moderately successful, but even by the early afternoon, as the fighting continued in the villages, the British were three hours behind schedule and in desperate need of the aerial support that the weather had denied them. Nevertheless, 11th Armoured Division had still to be unleashed and it was hoped that it would instil some much-needed momentum into the already stuttering offensive. (For further details about the advance of 15th Division's 44th and 46th Brigades see Tour A, *pages 125–46.*)

A Squadron, 2nd Northamptonshire Yeomanry (11th Armoured Division's reconnaissance regiment), was following behind 15th Division's leading units, along with 15th Division's 227th Brigade. The next phase of the plan was for 2nd Northamptonshire

A soldier from 8th Royal Scots takes up a firing position in a drainage ditch just outside la Gaule on 26 June. *(IWM B5960)*

Yeomanry to dash forward and seize the bridges over the Odon at Tourmauville and then Gavrus, while 15th Division's own reconnaissance regiment was to cover the left flank in the Mouen area. Meanwhile, 227th Brigade was to advance from Cheux, led by Churchill tanks from 7th and 9th RTR, and seize the line of the Caen–Villers-Bocage road (now the D675). Then, 10th Highland Light Infantry (HLI) and C Squadron, 7th RTR, were to take Grainville-sur-Odon and 2nd Gordons and C Squadron, 9th RTR, were to capture Tourville-sur-Odon. 2nd Argylls would then move forward and take over from 2nd Northamptonshire Yeomanry at the Odon bridges. The revised plan was for 2nd Argylls to reach the bridges by dark while other units of 29th Armoured Brigade were to prepare to push on to Hill 112 and the Orne in the next phase of the offensive.

Meanwhile, the Germans exploited the time that they had created for themselves, having fragmented the British attack that morning, to reinforce their defences north of the Odon. Thus, 5/, 7/ and 8/12th SS Panzer Regiment from the Rauray spur began taking up positions behind 26th SS Panzergrenadier Regiment south of Cheux in the general vicinity of Ring Contour 100. The 20-plus Panzer IVs began to arrive just as the British launched their push down to the Odon. In addition Dietrich released the Tiger I-equipped 3/101st Heavy SS Panzer Battalion, which moved into Grainville-sur-Odon during the afternoon. 21st Panzer Division also came to Meyer's aid with a company each of tanks and assault guns.

At about 1230 hours Roberts received orders to release 2nd Northamptonshire Yeomanry for its advance down to the Odon bridges. This spearhead was to be followed by 23rd Hussars on the left, 2nd Fife and Forfar Yeomanry on the right, and 3rd RTR in reserve. The Cromwell tanks of 2nd Northamptonshire Yeomanry advanced to Cheux but then came across a minefield that prevented them entering the village from the north. The sappers cleared what they could and the armour moved into Cheux (as 2nd Glasgow Highlanders continued in its efforts to clear it), immediately coming under fire from small arms, grenades and *Panzerfausts*. These delays allowed II/12th SS Panzers to complete its move from Rauray and meant that 2nd Northamptonshire Yeomanry missed the programmed supporting barrage that was to have supported its advance south from Cheux. Another delay was therefore incurred as another barrage was arranged.

Looking north over the ground near Norrey-en-Bessin over which 2nd Gordons advanced to la Gaule. Norrey-en-Bessin is to the right and le Mesnil-Patry is in the distance. *(Author)*

11th Armoured Division's armoured reconnaissance regiment, 2nd Northamptonshire Yeomanry, moving up towards Cheux during the late morning of 26 June in Cromwell cruiser tanks. *(IWM B5978)*

The attack then began with four troops of Northamptonshire Yeomanry Cromwells advancing astride the Cheux–Grainville-sur-Odon road (now the D170), but these quickly ran into the waiting German armour. Having trained with close infantry support, the British tankmen now found themselves isolated and exposed. During the exchange of fire that followed, both sides lost casualties, but No. 3 Troop of A Squadron was destroyed and Nos. 1 and

2 Troops were pinned down and unable to make any real progress. No. 4 Troop managed to advance in some dead ground, however, and reached the railway line at Grainville-sur-Odon at 1500 hours, but did not stay long before withdrawing. This was hardly the great armoured sweep that Lt-Gen O'Connor had envisaged making. 2nd Northamptonshire Yeomanry withdrew to lick its wounds and the hope of a swift *coup de main* to take the vital Odon bridges went with it.

As the armoured encounter was taking place on Ring Contour 100, 227th Brigade and the tanks from 29th Armoured Brigade moved forward to take up the challenge of pushing down to the Odon. The terrain was unlike that of the flat open countryside of East Anglia on which they had spent so long training, and there was only limited infantry support and no air cover. This was far from what those involved had expected, but the fog of war had descended heavily and they had to advance straight into it. The advance did not start well as, once again, there were significant problems just getting through Cheux.

Lt Steel Brownlie, 2nd Fife and Forfar Yeomanry, later said:

'The regiment formed up 1,000 yards short of Cheux alongside a regiment of Churchills from 31 Tank Brigade and an assault was made on the village. C Squadron went straight in. We went left but were stopped by tank ditches

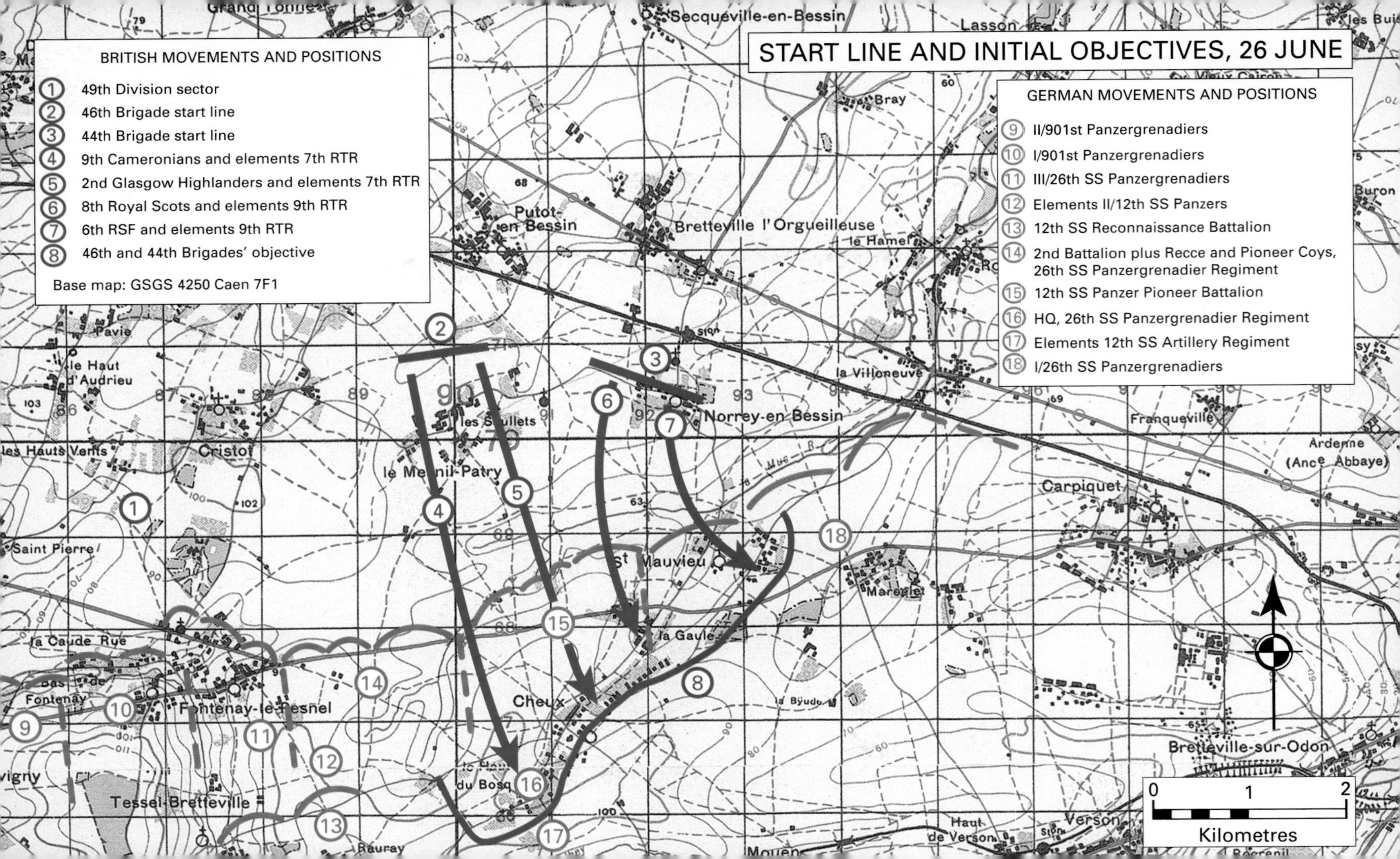
START LINE AND INITIAL OBJECTIVES, 26 JUNE
BRITISH MOVEMENTS AND POSITIONS
1 49th Division sector
2 46th Brigade start line
3 44th Brigade start line
4 9th Cameronians and elements 7th RTR
5 2nd Glasgow Highlanders and elements 7th RTR
6 8th Royal Scots and elements 9th RTR
7 6th RSF and elements 9th RTR
8 46th and 44th Brigades' objective
Base map: GSGS 4250 Caen 7F1
GERMAN MOVEMENTS AND POSITIONS
9 II/901st Panzergrenadiers
10 I/901st Panzergrenadiers
11 III/26th SS Panzergrenadiers
12 Elements II/12th SS Panzers
13 12th SS Reconnaissance Battalion
14 2nd Battalion plus Recce and Pioneer Coys, 26th SS Panzergrenadier Regiment
15 12th SS Panzer Pioneer Battalion
16 HQ, 26th SS Panzergrenadier Regiment
17 Elements 12th SS Artillery Regiment
18 I/26th SS Panzergrenadiers
Secqueville-en-Bessin
Lasson
Bray
Putot-en-Bessin
Bretteville l'Orgueilleuse
le Hamel
la Villeneuve
Norrey-en-Bessin
Franqueville
Ardenne
(Ance Abbaye)
Carpiquet
le Haut d'Audrieu
Pavie
Cristot
les Hauts Vents
les Saullets
le Mesnil-Patry
Saint Pierre
St Mauvieu
Marcelet
la Gaule
la Caude Rue
Bas de Fontenay
Fontenay-le-Pesnel
Cheux
la Byude
le Haut du Bosq
Tessel-Bretteville
Rauray
Haut de Verson
Verson
Bretteville-sur-Odon
Kilometres
0
1
2

and sunken lanes, so were switched to the right. Don Hall took his troop round the edge of a wood, myself following. Two of his tanks went up in flames and he came roaring back, laying smoke. I took cover but could not see anything because of the trees and smoke from the burning tanks. Two APs [armour-piercing rounds] came just over my head so I too laid smoke and got out.'

Source: quoted in Patrick Delaforce, *The Black Bull*, p. 31.

A Tiger tank (Panzer VI Mark E Tiger I) from 101st Heavy SS Panzer Battalion. The Tiger had a crew of five, weighed 56 tonnes and was armed with the formidable 88-mm gun and two 7.92-mm machine guns. *(IWM B6140)*

With observers on the Rauray ridge and Ring Contour 100, the Germans had seen the armour massing and II/12th SS Panzers and 12th SS Panzer Artillery Regiment opened up. The British armour attempted to bypass Cheux, but it seemed that wherever the tanks went, the Germans saw them. The tanks of C Squadron, 23rd Hussars, for example, skirted round Cheux to the east, on Ring

Contour 100. Four Shermans were hit by at least one of the Tigers that had just moved into the area north of Grainville-sur-Odon. Thus the advance by 29th Armoured Brigade faltered almost immediately, and revealed the skill and speed with which the Germans could react to an attack and plug the gaps in their line. This was not without cost to themselves, however, for the Germans suffered heavy casualties at the hands of the British tanks. Once they had rebuffed the advance, the Germans were forced to reorganise and redeploy – but they still dominated the ground and routes south of Cheux.

Ring Contour 100 looking south towards Grainville-sur-Odon. *(Author)*

As the armour tried to batter its way south, the units of 227th Brigade were desperately trying to follow to provide support but had been slowed themselves and did not reach their forming-up position north of Cheux until 1800 hours. Moving through Cheux after the briefest of pauses, 10th HLI was not the first British unit of the day to be hampered by traffic jams, ruins and sniper scares. The infantry were therefore forced to leave much of their heavier support equipment and weaponry behind in their trucks as the battalion pressed on.

Roland Jefferson, 8th Rifle Brigade, later wrote:

'We moved through the blasted ruins of Cheux and for the first time encountered being shelled ourselves. There was German sniper action and we had to seek these out and eliminate them. Perhaps for the first time I realized that there was a vast difference between the text book soldiering when we were winning the battles on the Yorkshire moors and the real thing we were now experiencing.'

Source: quoted in Patrick Delaforce, *The Black Bull*, p. 32.

By this time 10th HLI had been forced to part from its supporting armour, C Squadron, 7th RTR, but continued with its final approach to the start line, which lay south of le Haut du Bosq on the road to Grainville-sur-Odon. However, before the battalion got in position, it ran into some dug-in tanks of 5/ and 7/12th SS Panzer Regiment. Without armoured support, machine guns and mortars, it was difficult for 10th HLI to overcome them. After a period of confusion, the supporting Churchill tanks arrived and returned fire, but there was still no way of breaking the German position that evening with the light fading. After withdrawing to the southern outskirts of Cheux, 10th HLI's commanding officer, Lt-Col J.D.S. Young, prepared for a renewed advance the next morning.

Meanwhile, 2nd Gordons, supported by C Squadron, 9th RTR, formed up under *Nebelwerfer* fire east of Cheux and could see the positions of 7th Seaforths on the northern edge of Ring Contour 100. As 2nd Gordons began its advance towards Colleville and Tourville-sur-Odon, supported by a creeping barrage, dug-in tanks from II/12th SS Panzers, well-sited machine guns of 15th (Reconnaissance) Company, 25th SS Panzergrenadier Regiment, and some anti-tank guns caused considerable difficulties, and the rain and hail only made the conditions more unpleasant. Nevertheless, 2nd Gordons and 9th RTR pushed on across Ring Contour 100 and crossed the Ruisseau de Salbey stream, but men of 25th SS Panzergrenadiers inserted themselves between the two forward companies of 2nd Gordons and those companies following. A and B Companies pushed on up the ridge towards the woods with some armoured support; B Company made it to the edge of Colleville but A Company was caught in the open by mortar fire and suffered considerable casualties. When darkness fell, C and D Companies and the battalion headquarters were only about 1.5 km south of Cheux and so they set up a defensive position close to the road and dug in.

Meanwhile, the 2nd Gordons battlegroup continued to attack Colleville and was met by elements of 12th SS Panzer Reconnaissance Battalion, the company from 25th SS

Troops moving cautiously through St-Manvieu-Norrey on 26 June when a 'sniper scare' was still concentrating minds. Most of the 'snipers' were actually only isolated riflemen with standard weaponry and training. *(IWM B5962)*

Panzergrenadier Regiment and Tigers from 101st Heavy SS Panzer Battalion. The Churchills of 9th RTR suffered nine losses and the infantry struggled to make further progress through a hail of small-arms and mortar fire as darkness fell. The situation was hopeless and so the tanks and infantry withdrew in small groups. 2nd Gordons suffered over 100 casualties on 26 June.

Bill Thompson of 9th RTR has said:

'The first day my squadron lost 13 tanks out of 18; fortunately, a number of the tanks were recoverable and the loss among the crew was not too great but the first one killed in my regiment was Sidney Chapman, our Troop corporal... In that first action 'C' Squadron supported 1 Bn [*sic*] The Gordon Highlanders of the 15th Scottish and being half-Scots I was proud to be fighting alongside them. They took a lot of casualties and that night I remember

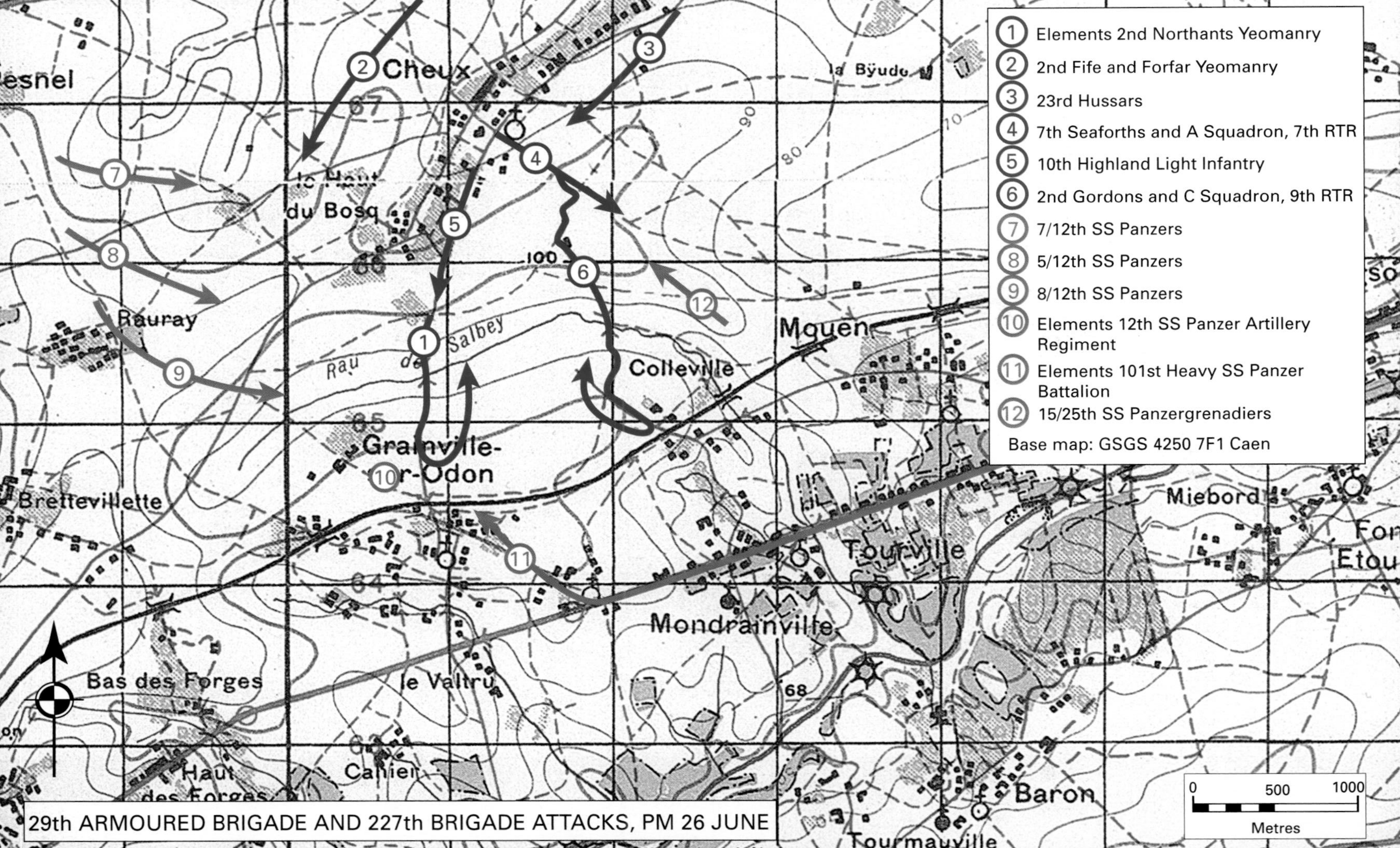

29th ARMOURED BRIGADE AND 227th BRIGADE ATTACKS, PM 26 JUNE

quite clearly the sound of bagpipes as the Gordons and the other Scots battalions played laments – 'Flowers of the Forest' – to honour their fallen. It made the hair stand up on the back of my neck.'

Source: quoted in Robin Neillands, *The Battle of Normandy*, pp. 165–6.

The village of Grainville-sur-Odon seen from the north-east. It was across this ground that 2nd Gordons and 9th RTR approached on the evening of 26 June and then attacked the following morning. *(Author)*

With the ending of the attack on Colleville during the evening of 26 June the British attacks finished, to be replaced by localised German counter-attacks. In those at St-Manvieu-Norrey, for example, infantry and tanks probed forward only to be repulsed. 6th RSF in the village was relieved by 6th King's Own Scottish Borderers (KOSB) that evening (less one company that went to reinforce 8th Royal Scots in la Gaule), and beat off another counter-attack on the village at 2000 hours.

Whilst 29th Armoured Brigade, 31st Tank Brigade and 227th Brigade were in action, 43rd Division moved forward to relieve 15th Division. 129th Brigade was to relieve 44th Brigade and 214th Brigade to relieve 46th Brigade so that the latter could move down to the Odon. A confused relief of the recently arrived 6th KOSB in St-Manvieu-Norrey by 4th Wiltshires was completed by midnight. During this time I/26th SS Panzergrenadiers, which had continued to fight in and around the village, was withdrawn, although its 1st and 3rd Companies continued to hold on to their positions on the right flank. In la Gaule, 5th Wiltshires had relieved 8th Royal Scots by 0300 hours on 27 June. 214th Brigade, meanwhile, moved forward to relieve 46th Brigade in Cheux and le Haut du Bosq. However, the transport of both 5th Duke of Cornwall's Light Infantry (DCLI) and 1st Worcesters got stuck in a traffic jam and this caused great delay. The result was that, by dawn on 27 June, 214th Brigade had not managed to relieve 46th Brigade.

A pause in the attack while a mortar barrage is fired on an unknown village on the morning of 26 June. *(IWM B5954)*

END OF THE DAY: 26 JUNE

The first day of Operation Epsom was not an outstanding success for Lt-Gen O'Connor, for the Odon had not even been reached, let alone crossed, but neither was it a great failure. The Germans had successfully fragmented and slowed the British advance; this, assisted by good observation, excellent prepared defensive positions and skilful troops, knocked the British behind schedule very early in the battle. Clearly the attackers were disadvantaged in a number of critical areas, none so important as the weather that stopped them taking advantage of their air power. Thus, when the attack was launched and so many troops and armoured assets were packed into such a small area with relatively open flanks and poor road communication against a well-prepared enemy in good defensive terrain, confusion, delay and a significant lack of momentum unsurprisingly followed.

Men of 6th Royal Scots Fusiliers during their clearing operations in St-Manvieu-Norrey on the early afternoon of 26 June. *(IWM B5966)*

The Germans were, however, destabilised by the attack and suffered significant casualties (including 730 from 12th SS Panzer Division). Nevertheless, at the end of 26 June they were still in possession of some strong and dominating positions on the vital high ground and had been able to plug holes in their defences. It was critical for a concerned Kurt Meyer and his *Hitlerjugend* Division to hold on for, as he was told by I SS Panzer Corps, 'Positions must be defended to the last cartridge! We have to fight

The transport for 7th Seaforths in a traffic jam caused by the fighting in Cheux on 26 June. *(IWM B5975)*

for time. II SS Panzer Corps is on its way to the front.' *Generalfeldmarschall* (Field Marshal) Erwin Rommel, commander of Army Group B and in overall tactical charge of the German force in Normandy, underlined this at 2100 hours by demanding that, 'everything which can be assembled must be thrown at the fight.' Thus, 2nd Panzer Division and 21st Panzer Division were each ordered to supply a battlegroup based on a tank battalion. Meanwhile, the leading element (Battlegroup *Weidinger*) of 2nd SS Panzer Division *Das Reich*, which had come from the south of France, and another battalion of 7th Projector Brigade's *Nebelwerfers* headed for the battlefield. Two panzergrenadier battalions from 1st SS Panzer Division *Leibstandarte-SS Adolf Hitler* were also *en route*, but they had been held up and were not expected to arrive before dawn, the rest of the division by 28 June and II SS Panzer Corps before 29 June. I SS Panzer Corps therefore planned to launch a counter-attack on 27 June and, at the very least, continue to hold back the British armour and infantry that had trickled south during the 26th.

27 June was, therefore, going to be a critical day for Operation Epsom. The British still had enormous assets with which to strike a devastating blow. As O'Connor knew only too well, though, time was of the essence, for he expected strong German counter-attacks at their earliest opportunity, as was their wont. The battle was still in the balance with the chance of both sides being able to influence it to their own advantage.

CHAPTER 3

27–28 JUNE

The German command was surprised, but relieved, that the British did not continue with their offensive during the night of 26/27 June. Under the cover of darkness Dietrich and Meyer set about reorganising their forces. By morning facing the renewed British onslaught were: I/ and II/26th SS Panzergrenadiers; the survivors of 12th SS Panzer Pioneer Battalion; about 30 Panzer IVs of II/12th SS Panzers; 12th SS Panzer Reconnaissance Battalion, to the north-west of Colleville; and approximately 12 Tigers of 2/ and 3/101st Heavy SS Panzer Battalion, operating in the area from Verson to Grainville-sur-Odon. On the right flank between Marcelet and Colleville were the weak tank and assault gun companies from 21st Panzer Division and on the high ground of the Rauray spur on the left flank were 17 Panthers of I/12th SS Panzers, some Panthers from 2nd Panzer Division, and infantry of III/26th SS Panzer-grenadiers. The 88-mm guns of 4th Anti-Aircraft Regiment remained to the rear.

The British also needed to reorganise during the night and Lt-Gen O'Connor changed the details of his plan to take account of events on the opening day. The new attacks on 27 June would, therefore, see 227th Infantry Brigade make another push down to the Odon to secure the bridges, supported by two regiments of 29th Armoured Brigade, namely 2nd Fife and Forfar Yeomanry and 23rd Hussars. 46th Brigade was to follow and relieve 227th Brigade in Colleville and Grainville so that 227th Brigade could then push further on. 44th Brigade was to be in reserve. Meanwhile, 11th Armoured Division was to cross the Odon after the bridges had been seized and create a bridgehead. Momentum was still essential – but the day dawned with drizzling rain and, therefore, no air support was immediately available to help with the accomplishment of this ambition.

27 June: Infantry warily approaching Cheux with 23rd Hussars. Dense woods, copses and hedges were common all over the battlefield and often contained concealed German positions. *(IWM B6147)*

49th Division continued its pressure on the Rauray spur on 27 June in order to dilute the available German forces that might otherwise be used to counter Epsom, and to take the critical high ground. Thus, before dawn, the Hallamshire Battalion established positions at the southern end of Tessel Wood, but an attack to reach Vendes failed. 11th DLI tried to infiltrate Rauray for most of the morning, supported by armour of 1st Nottinghamshire Yeomanry. The village, held by III/26th SS Panzergrenadiers with supporting tanks and 88-mm guns, was not taken, however. The attack resumed at 1400 hours and this time was a success; the men from 49th Division moved into the village and had cleared it by 1600 hours. The taking of this ground was of major benefit to Operation Epsom, as it denied the Germans an important area of observation over the battlefield, but the Germans still held other dominating positions

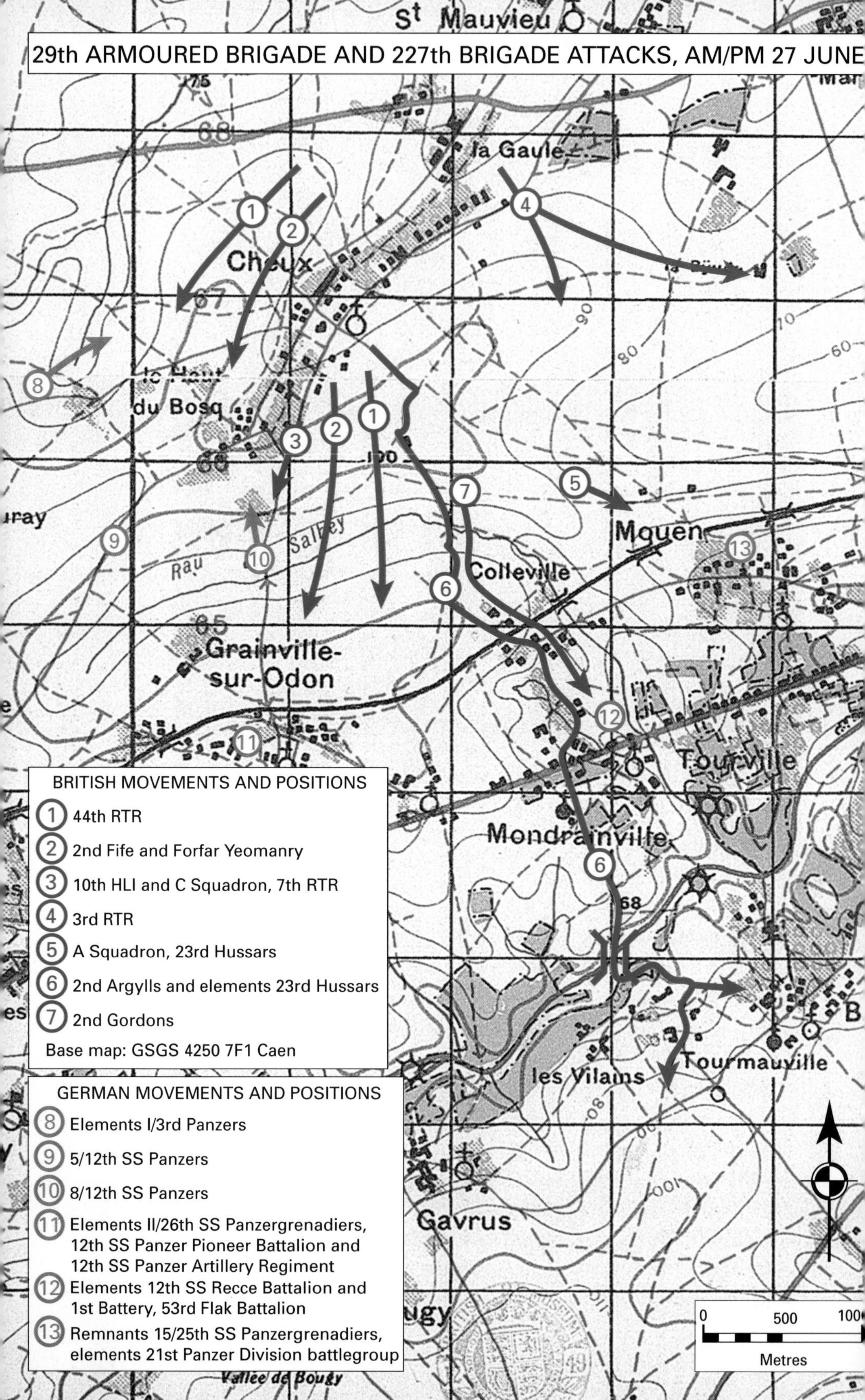

29th ARMOURED BRIGADE AND 227th BRIGADE ATTACKS, AM/PM 27 JUNE
St Mauvieu
la Gaule
Cheux
le Haut du Bosq
Mouen
Colleville
Grainville-sur-Odon
Tourville
Mondrainville
Tourmauville
les Vilains
Gavrus
Rau Salbey
Vallée de Bougy
BRITISH MOVEMENTS AND POSITIONS
1 44th RTR
2 2nd Fife and Forfar Yeomanry
3 10th HLI and C Squadron, 7th RTR
4 3rd RTR
5 A Squadron, 23rd Hussars
6 2nd Argylls and elements 23rd Hussars
7 2nd Gordons
Base map: GSGS 4250 7F1 Caen
GERMAN MOVEMENTS AND POSITIONS
8 Elements I/3rd Panzers
9 5/12th SS Panzers
10 8/12th SS Panzers
11 Elements II/26th SS Panzergrenadiers, 12th SS Panzer Pioneer Battalion and 12th SS Panzer Artillery Regiment
12 Elements 12th SS Recce Battalion and 1st Battery, 53rd Flak Battalion
13 Remnants 15/25th SS Panzergrenadiers, elements 21st Panzer Division battlegroup
0
500
Metres

on high ground further to the south. At 2100 hours, 1st Tyneside Scots moved up from an assembly point to the south of Fontenay-le-Pesnel in preparation for an attack on that ground at Brettevillette the following morning.

Men of 10th DLI by the side of a track, while a Sherman tank of 1st Notts Yeomanry and a despatch rider drive past, 28 June. *(IWM B6131)*

227th Brigade Attacks

As 49th Division pushed towards Rauray, 15th Division struck again on the Epsom battlefield. At 0445 hours 227th Brigade's 10th HLI launched an attack west of Cheux, along with tanks from 31st Tank Brigade, in an attempt to take the Gavrus crossing over the Odon. Then, at 0730 hours, 2nd Argylls attacked east of Cheux with the tanks of 23rd Hussars in order to take the bridge across the Odon at Tourmauville (for more detail on these events see Tour B, *pages 146–61*). 29th Armoured Brigade was to be ready to follow up 227th Brigade's success and 11th Armoured Division's 159th Brigade was to advance via the Odon crossings and establish bridgeheads.

10th HLI advanced from the Cheux–Grainville-sur-Odon road just south of le Haut du Bosq, the scene of the battalion's failure the previous day, after a heavy preliminary bombardment. The attack immediately ran into 8/12th SS Panzers, with only four serviceable Panzer IVs, supported by remnants of II/26th SS Panzer-grenadiers, 12th SS Panzer Pioneer Battalion and I and II/12th SS Panzer Artillery. The battle was ferocious and bloody with both sides taking heavy casualties, but again the Germans held firm and no progress could be made. There is no doubt that this failure was a set-back to the plans, but as the fighting continued throughout the day, it did pin the Germans to the area immediately south of Cheux. 10th HLI suffered 112 casualties on 27 June.

The fixing of the Germans by 10th HLI gave 2nd Argylls an opportunity to advance relatively unmolested later that morning. The battalion moved through the position to which 2nd Gordons had withdrawn on the previous day near the Salbey, and then pushed on to Colleville. The weakened German forces in the village fought tenaciously and caused considerable casualties with their well positioned 88-mm guns. The fighting in the village lasted into the afternoon. Nevertheless, the firepower of 2nd Argylls and 23rd Hussars, assisted by the artillery, eventually overcame the defenders and the infantry seized control of the village and then cleared it. At last VIII Corps had a springboard from which it could launch its attacks on the Odon – albeit 24 hours behind schedule.

Once relieved during the previous night, 44th Brigade had gone into divisional reserve in the area of le Mesnil-Patry, but by dawn 43rd Division's 214th Brigade had failed to relieve 46th Brigade in Cheux and le Haut du Bosq. This prevented 44th Brigade, less 7th Seaforths, from being available for the push forward early that morning. 5th DCLI from 214th Brigade had set out to relieve 9th Cameronians in the northern part of le Haut du Bosq at 0200 hours. When 5th DCLI got there, however, it found that 9th Cameronians had already left and German riflemen had filled the village. Then, after digging in to the west of the village, elements of 5th DCLI were flushing the Germans out of le Haut du Bosq when they were engaged by tanks from I/3rd Panzers of 2nd Panzer Division, which had advanced from Rauray at 0930 hours. Six Panthers broke into the battalion positions and killed the commanding officer, Lt-Col P. Atherton, before one tank fled, one turned over and another four, amazingly, were knocked out by PIATs. Other elements of the German battlegroup grappled with

10th HLI to the south and were engaged and repelled by 7th RTR and 44th RTR.

Meanwhile, the main body of German tanks advanced towards Cheux, where 214th Brigade's 1st Worcesters had relieved 2nd Gordons that morning. These Panthers were stopped by the Royal Artillery's 17-pounders. The 2nd Panzer Division battlegroup's counter-attack had failed, but it had disrupted 227th Brigade's plans.

South of Cheux, 7th Seaforths, which had been unable to take the crest of Ring Contour 100 the previous evening, was able to capture this piece of high ground after its defenders withdrew, having found themselves outflanked by 2nd Argylls' attack on Colleville. As 2nd Argylls pressed on to the Odon, supported by 23rd Hussars, 2nd Gordons had advanced into Colleville and then moved south to Tourville-sur-Odon. 2nd Gordons was replaced in Colleville by 7th Seaforths, which was then in turn relieved by 2nd Glasgow Highlanders.

The top of Ring Contour 100, looking north, with Cheux on the left and la Gaule in the centre. *(Author)*

As 2nd Argylls moved into Colleville, 29th Armoured Brigade had also moved forward from Cheux, with 2nd Fife and Forfar Yeomanry pushing down towards Grainville-sur-Odon and 3rd RTR towards Mouen. 44th RTR of 4th Armoured Brigade also advanced near le Haut du Bosq. One company of 101st Heavy SS Panzer Battalion's Tigers opened up from the area of Mouen, briefly

D Company, 7th Seaforths, advancing to contact with the enemy. *(IWM B6003)*

checking both 3rd RTR and 2nd Fife and Forfar Yeomanry, but the advances continued. Nevertheless, 2nd Fife and Forfar Yeomanry's entry to Grainville was blocked by some isolated groups of SS panzergrenadiers and 8/12th SS Panzers, which had withdrawn from the south of le Haut du Bosq that afternoon when it looked as though they were becoming isolated, and some of the 101st Heavy SS Panzer Battalion's Tigers that had moved to the left flank.

However, following 2nd Glasgow Highlanders into Colleville, 9th Cameronians, mounted on 7th RTR tanks, then advanced to Grainville. The Cameronians' D Company attacked, supported by the battalion anti-tank platoon, but could not clear the village before nightfall. The British attack was, therefore, brought to an end and plans made for a renewed effort the following dawn.

The Germans were by that time just holding on in the area north of the Odon, as 227th Brigade and 29th Armoured Brigade continued their advance towards the Caen–Villers-Bocage road. In this move the tanks of 23rd Hussars crashed their way forward in support of 2nd Argylls, with B Squadron moving north-west of Mondrainville to engage targets to the south of the Odon while other parts of the regiment continued towards the river with the infantry.

As 2nd Argylls advanced south of the Caen–Villers-Bocage road it ran into patrols from 12th SS Panzer Reconnaissance Battalion and some isolated tanks, which were swept aside. Advancing with open flanks and not entirely sure what the Germans had waiting for it, the British battlegroup probed forward down towards the Odon. 2nd Argylls seized the Tourmauville bridge at around 1700 hours and a small bridgehead was established, which was then strengthened by elements of 23rd Hussars.

The Tourmauville bridge over the Odon from the south bank of the river. *(Author)*

On arrival at the Odon C Squadron, 23rd Hussars, crossed the bridge, moved through Tourmauville and then fanned out in defensive positions. Following them was 11th Armoured Division's 159th Brigade, which was to consolidate and enlarge the bridgehead. 159th Brigade's move forward was handled extremely poorly, however, with too little information being given to the battalions and too much speed demanded as the light began to fail. The result was that C Company of 3rd Monmouths got lost and ended up in Mouen – where it spent the night – while the rest of the battalion followed 1st Herefords and 4th King's Shropshire

Light Infantry (KSLI) as they moved over the Odon and into the bridgehead to take up defensive positions.

As darkness fell and British troops tentatively established themselves south of the Odon, in the middle of the battlefield there remained considerable confusion as so many troops and vehicles were packed into a small area with extremely limited road communication. Such difficulties did not augur well for operations on the following day. Nevertheless, the British forces were at last achieving some momentum and had a springboard from which they could launch attacks beyond the Odon. Even so, the flanks were still vulnerable and at its head the salient – now known as the 'Scottish Corridor' – was extremely narrow. It was therefore crucial that the salient be filled out and the front pushed further south of the Odon.

The officers' mess truck of 2nd Fife and Forfar Yeomanry travelling through Cheux on 27 June. *(IWM B6039)*

For the Germans, of course, it was important that they moved into blocking positions and launched counter-attacks to stifle VIII Corps. Thus, during the night, Meyer moved his own headquarters to Louvigny, redeployed the armour on the Rauray spur to Hill 112 and established defensive positions along the line from

Carpiquet airfield (an attack against which had been postponed by the Canadians) to Verson, Fontaine-Étoupefour, Hill 112, Esquay-Notre-Dame, Gavrus and Grainville-sur-Odon and finally to Brettevillette. Everything that could be thrown into this line was, including gunners with no guns, lines of communication troops, tanks from 21st Panzer Division, *Luftwaffe* anti-aircraft personnel and the mortar battalion from 83rd Projector Regiment. Also during that night, the vanguard of 1st SS Panzer Division arrived. This battlegroup, commanded by *SS-Obersturmbannführer* (Lt-Col) Albert Frey, came under Meyer's command. It was immediately ordered to counter-attack westwards out of Verson the following day and link up with Battlegroup *Weidinger*, from 2nd SS Panzer Division, in the Grainville-sur-Odon area.

As Meyer sought to deal directly with the British offensive, at 0810 hours on 28 June, *Generaloberst* (Colonel-General) Friedrich Dollmann's Seventh Army HQ ordered *SS-Obergruppenführer* (Lt-Gen) Paul Hausser's II SS Panzer Corps to the Odon front, to 'attack immediately in order to clear the breach south of Cheux'. As only elements of the corps were in the vicinity, Hausser replied that he was not able to attack before the following day. At this (and under great and growing pressure), Dollmann committed suicide. Thus, at a vital stage in Epsom, the Germans were forced that afternoon into a series of changes in command appointments with Hausser taking command of Seventh Army and *SS-Obergruppenführer* Willi Bittrich, the commander of 9th SS Panzer Division, taking his job at II SS Panzer Corps. Both I and II SS Panzer Corps were to come under command of *General der Panzertruppen* (General of Armoured Troops) Leo Freiherr Geyr von Schweppenburg's Panzer Group West, along with XLVII Panzer Corps and LXXXVI Corps. II SS Panzer Corps was, meanwhile, to prepare for a counter-attack against VIII Corps on the morning of 29 June on a line running from Noyers-Bocage to Bougy.

Whilst such important decisions were being taken, the battle continued. 49th Division successfully captured Point 110 that afternoon and just managed to hold on to it after Battlegroup *Weidinger* counter-attacked. With the taking of this high ground, and with Rauray already in British hands in spite of the continued fight for Brettevillette, the British had at last denied the Germans their magnificent observation over the Epsom battlefield. In getting there, they had diluted the German resources that might have been placed in the way of VIII Corps.

While this was going on, attempts were made to push out of the Odon bridgehead and seize Hill 112 but, in order to facilitate this, considerable work had to be undertaken north of the Odon to open up routes from Grainville-sur-Odon to Gavrus and to consolidate the area from Colleville to Tourmauville.

Wounded German prisoners from 12th SS Panzer Division being escorted back behind British lines on 28 June. *(IWM B6008)*

With 2nd Argylls preparing to move towards the Gavrus bridges during 28 June, it was critical that Grainville-sur-Odon was captured and a route cleared down the west side of the corridor to the river. Thus, at 0530 hours 9th Cameronians and 7th RTR renewed their attack on Grainville, which was successful at 1300 hours after some close-quarter street fighting and accurate artillery support. German counter-attacks followed, during which 9th Cameronians suffered heavy casualties, but Grainville remained in Scottish hands.

Meanwhile, in an attempt to start the push from Grainville down to Gavrus, 7th Seaforths, commanded by Lt-Col E.H.G. Grant, set off from Cheux, crossed Ring Contour 100 and then headed south for Colleville, which provided the only crossing point over the railway for tracked vehicles (the line ran through a deep cutting across the Epsom battlefield). The battalion then successfully took le Valtru with Churchill tanks in support. Having made contact with 9th Cameronians on the right and 2nd Glasgow Highlanders on the left, 7th Seaforths dug in. Both Grainville and le Valtru were hit hard by artillery fire directed from the Rauray spur, however, before that high ground was cleared by 49th Division. 9th Cameronians in Grainville and 7th Seaforths in le Valtru were also, as we shall see, engaged by Battlegroup *Weidinger* that afternoon.

That same afternoon, a little further to the south and east, 2nd Argylls' commanding officer, Lt-Col John W. Tweedie, pushed two fighting patrols out of the Tourmauville bridgehead, which seized the Gavrus bridges unopposed and intact. During the remaining daylight hours, the rest of the battalion followed on an exhausting journey along the dense countryside offered by the south bank of the Odon. 2nd Argylls reached Gavrus intact, however, and immediately set up a defensive bridgehead position to the south of the river.

The le Valtru crossroads, looking east. Gavrus is to the right; Mondrainville is straight on and Grainville-sur-Odon is to the left. *(Author)*

With 46th Brigade having expanded the western side of the corridor by taking Grainville-sur-Odon and le Valtru, 44th Brigade moved forward from Cheux to add greater depth and strength to

Top left: Officers atop a 7th RTR Churchill tank on 28 June. Seated on the turret are (*left*) Lt-Col R. Delacombe, 8th Royal Scots, and Lt-Col G. Gainsford, 7th RTR. *(IWM B6113)*

Top right: A Churchill tank of 7th RTR and men of 8th Royal Scots move cautiously through a hedgerow on 28 June. *(IWM B6123)*

Main picture: A lorry explodes on the Epsom battlefield. *(IWM B6017)*

2nd Glasgow Highlanders advancing through a cornfield with 7th RTR on 28 June. *(IWM B6119)*

the position. Thus, at 1400 hours, 6th KOSB relieved 10th HLI, which was still dug-in south of Cheux. That evening, 8th Royal Scots came up on the right and 2nd Northamptonshire Yeomanry on the left, both units moving forward towards Grainville and stopping about a kilometre short of the village at dusk. By the end of 28 June, therefore, the British forces had made significant progress around the Caen–Villers-Bocage road near Grainville, but 2nd Argylls was still isolated and the Germans continued to dominate the road south to Gavrus and also north of Grainville back to Cheux.

Meanwhile, that morning, a German counter-attack was launched from Verson in the east and Noyers-Bocage in the west. Battlegroup *Weidinger*, attacking from the west, comprised I/4th SS Panzergrenadier Regiment *Der Führer*, plus the pioneer, infantry gun, reconnaissance and anti-aircraft companies of that regiment, and I/3rd SS Panzergrenadier Regiment *Deutschland*. Both these regiments were from 2nd SS Panzer Division. The SS battlegroup was assisted by some Panthers from I/3rd Panzer Regiment. The exact composition of Frey's force on the east flank is not known but probably included I/ and II/1st SS Panzergrenadier Regiment; five Panzer IVs of 4/22nd Panzers and five Panthers from I/12th SS Panzer Regiment; possibly three Tigers from 101st Heavy SS Panzer Battalion; and a battalion of 83rd Projector Regiment. Frey feared, however, that he lacked essential artillery support but was advised that the guns of 12th SS Panzer Division would support the attack.

A German sniping platform on the Epsom battlefield, 29 June. *(IWM B5216)*

Frey's attack began at 0600 hours, I/1st SS Panzergrenadiers on the right and II/1st SS Panzergrenadiers on the left leading the armour towards Colleville. I/1st SS Panzergrenadiers soon became embroiled in fighting on the northern outskirts of Mouen around the railway line against the lost company of 3rd Monmouths and the Panzer IVs with the Stuart tanks of 3rd County of London Yeomanry's reconnaissance troop. On the left, II/1st SS Panzergrenadiers advanced into Mouen and the area of Tourville-sur-Odon. There was no artillery support from 12th SS Panzer Division as had been promised and this allowed local British counter-attacks to disrupt Frey's intentions with relative impunity.

Frey later wrote:

'The enemy offered immediate and heavy resistance. A remarkable feature of the resistance was the machine gun fire. It was very heavy and fell with equal intensity along the entire attack sector.'

Source: quoted in Rudolf Lehmann and Ralf Tiemann, *The Leibstandarte*, Vol. 4, Pt. 1, page 121.

Nevertheless, with the Germans putting pressure on 2nd Glasgow Highlanders in Colleville and its vital road connection with the Odon, the British needed to make a concerted effort against the battlegroup. Therefore, at 1945 hours, an attack by 10th HLI, supported by a squadron of Shermans from 3rd County of London Yeomanry, engaged Battlegroup *Frey*'s northern flank. Although it failed to retake Mouen, this British attack did stall further German progress and initiated some fighting that continued through the night. Frey had failed to cut the corridor, but he had taken a bite out of what little width the salient had. In response 43rd Division was ordered forward to clear up the British left flank and strengthen positions there in advance of the counter-attack by II SS Panzer Corps which was now expected.

As Frey flung his force at the eastern side of the corridor, Weidinger did the same from the west, with the main objective being Mondrainville. I/3rd SS Panzergrenadiers attacked on the left against Brettevillette while on the right, I/4th SS Panzergrenadiers advanced towards Grainville-sur-Odon, with Panthers supporting both assaults. At Brettevillette, 1st Tyneside Scottish, supported by the Shermans of 4th/7th Royal Dragoon Guards, clashed with I/3rd SS Panzergrenadiers and 11th Durham Light Infantry was engaged on Point 110. After some confused fighting in which the British lost and then retook ground, the Germans were held with heavy casualties on both sides. On Weidinger's right, along the main road to Caen, I/4th SS Panzergrenadiers came under fire from 9th Cameronians in Grainville to the north and then ran into 7th Seaforth Highlanders at le Valtru to the south. Both British battalions, supported by 9th RTR, held their ground in what was, after all, good defensive countryside. Even so, some Panthers managed to infiltrate between Grainville and le Valtru, but were stopped by heavy and accurate British artillery fire. With this, Weidinger's counter-attack petered out and, although coming within just a kilometre of meeting up with the tip of Battlegroup *Frey*

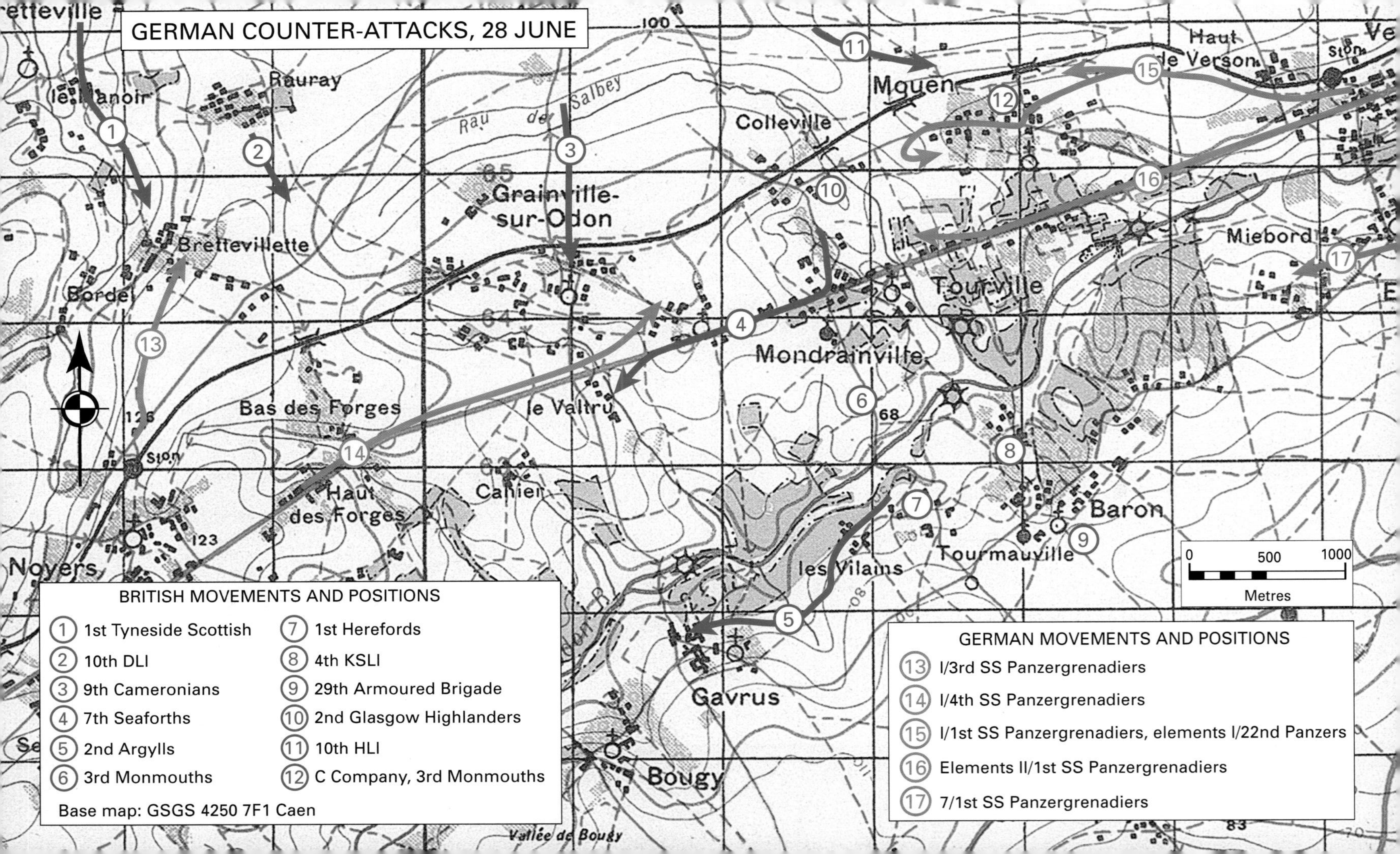
GERMAN COUNTER-ATTACKS, 28 JUNE
BRITISH MOVEMENTS AND POSITIONS
1 1st Tyneside Scottish
2 10th DLI
3 9th Cameronians
4 7th Seaforths
5 2nd Argylls
6 3rd Monmouths
7 1st Herefords
8 4th KSLI
9 29th Armoured Brigade
10 2nd Glasgow Highlanders
11 10th HLI
12 C Company, 3rd Monmouths
Base map: GSGS 4250 7F1 Caen
GERMAN MOVEMENTS AND POSITIONS
13 I/3rd SS Panzergrenadiers
14 I/4th SS Panzergrenadiers
15 I/1st SS Panzergrenadiers, elements I/22nd Panzers
16 Elements II/1st SS Panzergrenadiers
17 7/1st SS Panzergrenadiers
0
500
1000
Metres
le Manoir
Rauray
Brettevillette
Bordel
Grainville-sur-Odon
Rau de Salbey
Colleville
Mouen
Haut de Verson
Miebord
Tourville
Mondrainville
le Valtru
Bas des Forges
Haut des Forges
Cahier
Noyers
Baron
Tourmauville
les Vilains
Gavrus
Bougy
Vallée de Bougy

around Colleville, never had the power to break through in a meaningful fashion.

While the Germans attacked the flanks of the corridor, 29th Armoured Brigade was still attempting to push out of the Odon bridgehead and take Hill 112 to the south-east and Hill 113 to the south-west. That morning B Squadron, 23rd Hussars, headed off for Hill 112. This feature was held by some 12th SS Panzer Division panzergrenadiers and, around it, a *Luftwaffe* motorised anti-aircraft battery using its 88-mm guns in a ground role. B Squadron began its climb up the low ridge from the Odon valley from the north, coming under fire from the woods on the hilltop, from the west from dug-in tanks and 88-mm guns around Esquay-Notre-Dame and from the east by German guns in the Fontaine-Étoupefour area. Rocket-firing Typhoon fighter-bombers were called on to assist in the destruction of the guns and dug-in tanks, but without success. B Squadron lost several Shermans; a little later it was joined on the north slopes by C Squadron along with regimental HQ, some replacement tanks from 270th Forward Delivery Squadron and H Company, 8th Rifle Brigade. The British battlegroup established itself firmly on the hill, but the German guns continued to take their toll.

A Panther is approached by a Loyd Carrier, which is towing a 6-pounder anti-tank gun and transporting its crew. *(IWM B6045)*

Men of 8th Royal Scots moving forward on 28 June past a Humber scout car. *(IWM B6115)*

At this point H Company, 8th Rifle Brigade, commanded by Major Kenneth Mackenzie, attacked the woods on the crest, prompting approximately 70 panzergrenadiers and the anti-tank gunners to withdraw. Hill 112 had been taken, but there was no time for self-congratulation; the position was soon under extremely heavy bombardment and elements of both battalions of 12th SS Panzer Regiment counter-attacked up the southern and south-western slopes of the hill. Although the counter-attack that afternoon was rebuffed by a mixture of tank and anti-tank guns, the Germans had made it clear that any further movement forward would surely be met by their armour and 88-mm guns.

During the afternoon, 23rd Hussars was relieved by 3rd RTR and G Company, 8th Rifle Brigade, moving up from Baron-sur-Odon. They, too, tried to dislodge the German dug-in tanks and 88-mm guns on their right, but also failed. During 28 June some 40 Shermans were lost on Hill 112 and the British force was treated to a bombardment by every German gun in range. Meanwhile, an attempt by 44th RTR to take Hill 113 failed when it was stopped by German anti-tank guns. At dusk the Germans mounted another

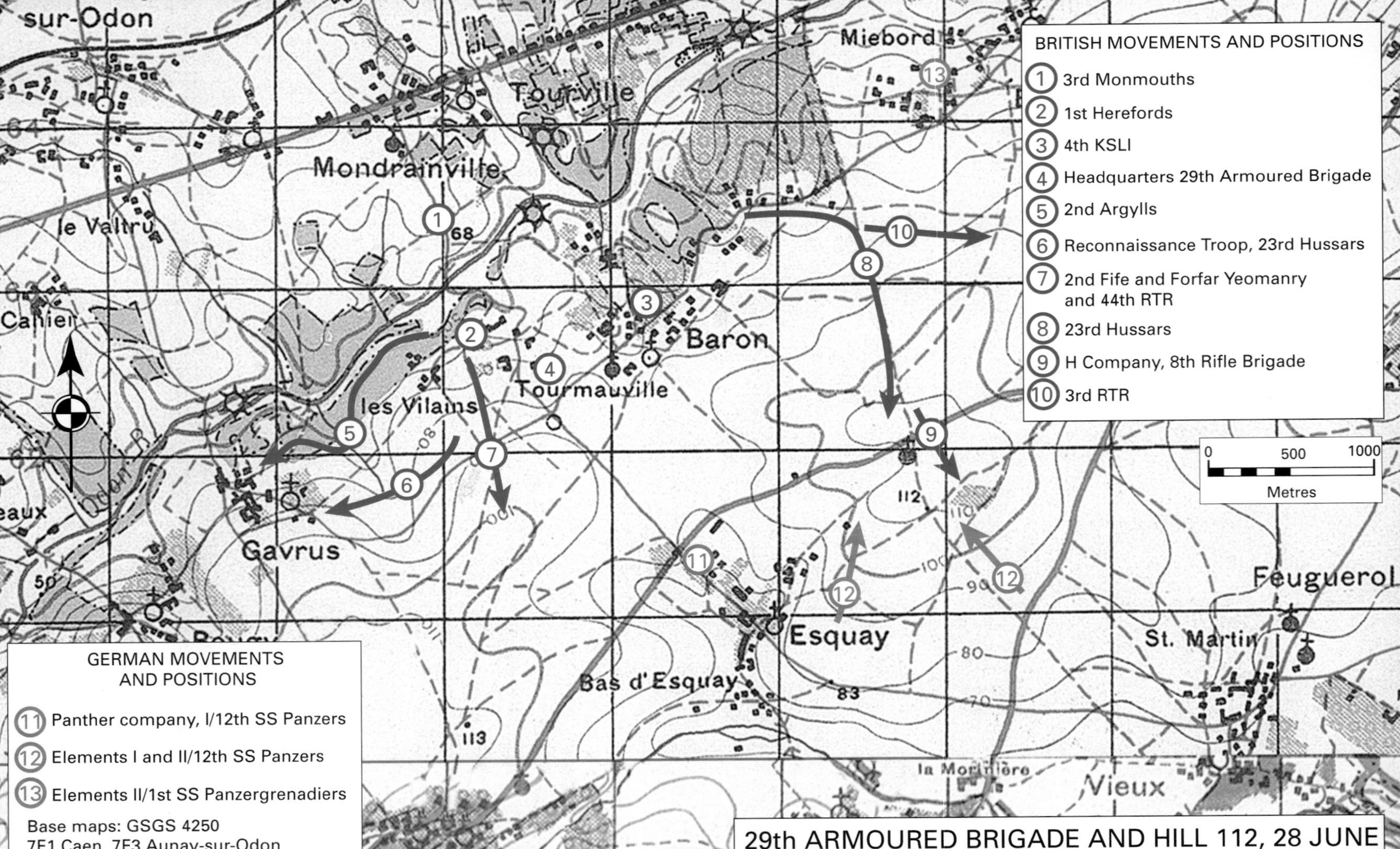

29th ARMOURED BRIGADE AND HILL 112, 28 JUNE

counter-attack on Hill 112, with tanks supported by panzer-grenadiers advancing from Esquay-Notre-Dame. The British artillery tried to break up this thrust without success, and G Company, 8th Rifle Brigade, was forced to withdraw and surrender the summit to the Germans once more.

The British position on the northern edge of Hill 112 was secure, even if it was hellish for those who remained there. Nevertheless, it should be remembered that 29th Armoured Brigade was surrounded on three sides and at the end of an extremely narrow corridor, with flanks that remained vulnerable. During the day Montgomery, Dempsey and O'Connor discussed reports based on Ultra code-breaking intelligence, which revealed that II SS Panzer Corps was closing towards the Epsom battlefield and was to attack in the west with the intention of destroying VIII Corps. These senior commanders had to decide how to use this information. Their decision was to ensure that the corridor could withstand the counter-attack before 11th Armoured Division continued its attack towards the Orne.

The day had started hopefully with the Odon crossed and a springboard for further offensive action established. However, preying on the minds of the commanders on 28 June was the feeling

Young German prisoners somewhere on the Epsom battlefield on 28 June. The badges on the left sleeves of two of the prisoners reveal that their rank is *Gefreiter* (lance-corporal). *(IWM B6174)*

that the Germans would have been assembling the resources for a counter-attack. Thus, although slight progress was made south of the Odon and positions were established on Hill 112, there was no exploitation to the Orne and 11th Armoured Division remained hemmed in. Moreover, with a narrow salient having been created in the push to the Odon, the vulnerable flanks were enticing for the Germans and much effort was put into fending off their unwelcome advances. Thus, by the end of the day, there was something of an impasse, with the British having been unable to push further than the crest of Hill 112 and the Germans having failed to cut the corridor. Nevertheless, the initiative seems to have been with the Germans, for their attacks had managed to slow the tempo of the British offensive enough to give themselves valuable time in which to launch II SS Panzer Corps in a counter-stroke that would force the British onto the back foot. Nevertheless, it could be argued that, by the end of 28 June, although little more ground had been taken, it was more firmly held and VIII Corps was in a better position than previously to withstand any counter-attack that appeared to be imminent. That night, 28/29 June, VIII Corps prepared to meet the might of II SS Panzer Corps head on.

CHAPTER 4

29–30 JUNE

On the morning of 29 June, the British aims for the day were to ensure the survivability of their bridgehead, consolidate their existing gains and prepare to meet the expected counter-attack by II SS Panzer Corps. Thus, on the battlefield, the Odon bridgehead

Churchills of 7th RTR on 28 June during the German counter-attack. *(IWM B6114)*

needed to be expanded: 15th Division had to clear the general area Colleville–Tourville–Tourmauville–Gavrus–Bougy Woods and defend its right flank. 43rd Division was to clear the area Bas de Mouen–Gournay and defend the left flank. Only when the salient had been made secure was 11th Armoured Division to continue its advance to the River Orne. There was a great advantage on this day, however, as aerial support became possible owing to a break in the weather.

Tidying Up the Scottish Corridor

Elements of 3rd Monmouths had occupied Mouen before it was lost during Frey's counter-attack from Verson on the previous day, and 10th HLI had been unable to retake it that evening. 214th Brigade of 43rd Division had moved forward to retake the village at 2000 hours on 28 June, but with limited daylight remaining and 10th HLI still engaged, the attack was postponed until the following morning. At 0800 hours on 29 June, 1st Worcesters attacked across the open cornfields on the extreme east flank of the corridor, supported by 179th Field Regiment, RA, and the divisional artillery, but no armour. Although there had been very little time to reconnoitre in daylight and develop a plan before H-Hour, the attack was a great success, with 1st Worcesters sticking close to the barrage. In the battle with the panzergrenadiers and tanks of

Battlegroup *Frey*, the going was slow due to the *bocage*. Nevertheless, Mouen was taken at 1100 hours and then 7th Somersets moved through 1st Worcesters to take up a strong position on the Caen–Villers-Bocage road.

With Mouen in British hands, 43rd Division's 129th Brigade advanced from St-Manvieu-Norrey with the task of clearing the woods and orchards between Tourville-sur-Odon and Baron-sur-Odon. With 5th Wiltshires on the right, 4th Somersets on the left, and supported by a squadron of 4th Armoured Brigade's Royal Scots Greys, the battalions advanced between Mouen and Colleville under heavy mortar fire until they reached the Caen–Villers-Bocage road. Here they reorganised before descending into the Odon valley and, having forged their own crossings over the river, began clearing the southern bank, north of Baron-sur-Odon. Meanwhile, 159th Brigade of 11th Armoured Division further expanded and strengthened the bridgehead with 3rd Monmouths just north of the Tourmauville bridge, 1st Herefords just to the south and 4th Shropshires clearing the area to the north-west of Baron-sur-Odon.

The Odon valley, taken to the south of Tourville-sur-Odon and looking across towards Baron-sur-Odon and Hill 112. *(Author)*

As the left flank was being cleared and the bridgehead was being reinforced, 15th Division's 44th Brigade began to tidy up the right flank of the Scottish Corridor. Critical in this was the widening of the narrow salient. Accordingly, at 1040 hours 8th Royal Scots moved forward from the position that it had secured with 6th

KOSB the previous evening just short of Grainville-sur-Odon, and dug in near the railway line to the north-west of the town. Then 6th RSF advanced towards the Caen–Villers-Bocage road and on further south towards the Gavrus bridges in an attempt to link up with the isolated 2nd Argylls. As 6th RSF was advancing, however, 8th Royal Scots was attacked. 6th RSF was ordered to help deal with this threat and thus failed to complete the consolidation of the right flank and 2nd Argylls remained alone on the Odon. 46th Brigade was, however, well set: 9th Cameronians was in Grainville-sur-Odon, 7th Seaforths in le Valtru and 2nd Glasgow Highlanders, having been relieved in Colleville that morning by 10th HLI, in Mondrainville.

The village of Grainville-sur-Odon as seen looking east from an area between le Valtru and Mondrainville. *(Author)*

HILLS 113 AND 112

With the Scottish Corridor being reorganised, the armour sought to strengthen the Odon bridgehead by seizing Hill 113. Thus, at 0910 hours, 4th Armoured Brigade's 44th RTR, supported by part of 2nd KRRC – both of which were under the command of 29th Armoured Brigade – began its attack. At the very same time, however, newly-arrived armoured units of 10th SS Panzer Division were preparing for their own. The two sides clashed before the British had reached their objective, but also before the Germans had reached Gavrus. 44th RTR withdrew back into defensive positions in the western section of the bridgehead – II SS Panzer Corps had begun making an impact.

While 44th RTR was starting its advance, elements of 29th Armoured Brigade once again fought for Hill 112. In this renewed battle, although elements of 3rd RTR failed to take Esquay-Notre-Dame after being engaged by six Tigers from 1/101st Heavy SS Panzer Battalion, other parts of 3rd RTR, supported by G and H Companies of 8th Rifle Brigade, advanced to retake the woods on Hill 112. They were immediately pummelled by a massive German bombardment.

The British efforts to strengthen their positions during the morning of 29 June were mirrored by those of II SS Panzer Corps, desperately trying to mass its forces for a counter-attack. More accurate and timely intelligence on German movements became available to the British senior commanders that morning, which revealed that the German armour sought to take the Baron-sur-Odon–Mouen–Cheux area and to destroy the British south of the Caen–Villers-Bocage road. Consequently, VIII Corps halted its offensive actions and ordered both 4th and 29th Armoured Brigades out of the Odon bridgehead. This meant, of course, not only pulling 3rd RTR off Hill 112, but also concentrating the two brigades at the rear of the corridor as a reserve. The bridgehead was to be held by 159th Brigade and the withdrawal covered by 2nd Northamptonshire Yeomanry. In this way VIII Corps prepared itself for the onslaught of the first major German counter-attack since the invasion had begun. The British had given away the offensive initiative.

The order given to II SS Panzer Corps was to 'attack on both sides of the Odon river towards the north-east in order to destroy the south-eastward penetrating enemy and clear the Villers-Bocage–Caen highway.' The German plan was, therefore, to attack from the west. 9th SS Panzer Division would attack on the left with Battlegroup *Weidinger*, its objectives to include Grainville-sur-Odon, Mouen, Cheux and Carpiquet airfield. 10th SS Panzer Division was to attack on the right and take Gavrus, Baron-sur-Odon, Hill 112 and Verson. The dividing line between the two divisions was the Odon. Meanwhile, elements of 12th SS Panzer

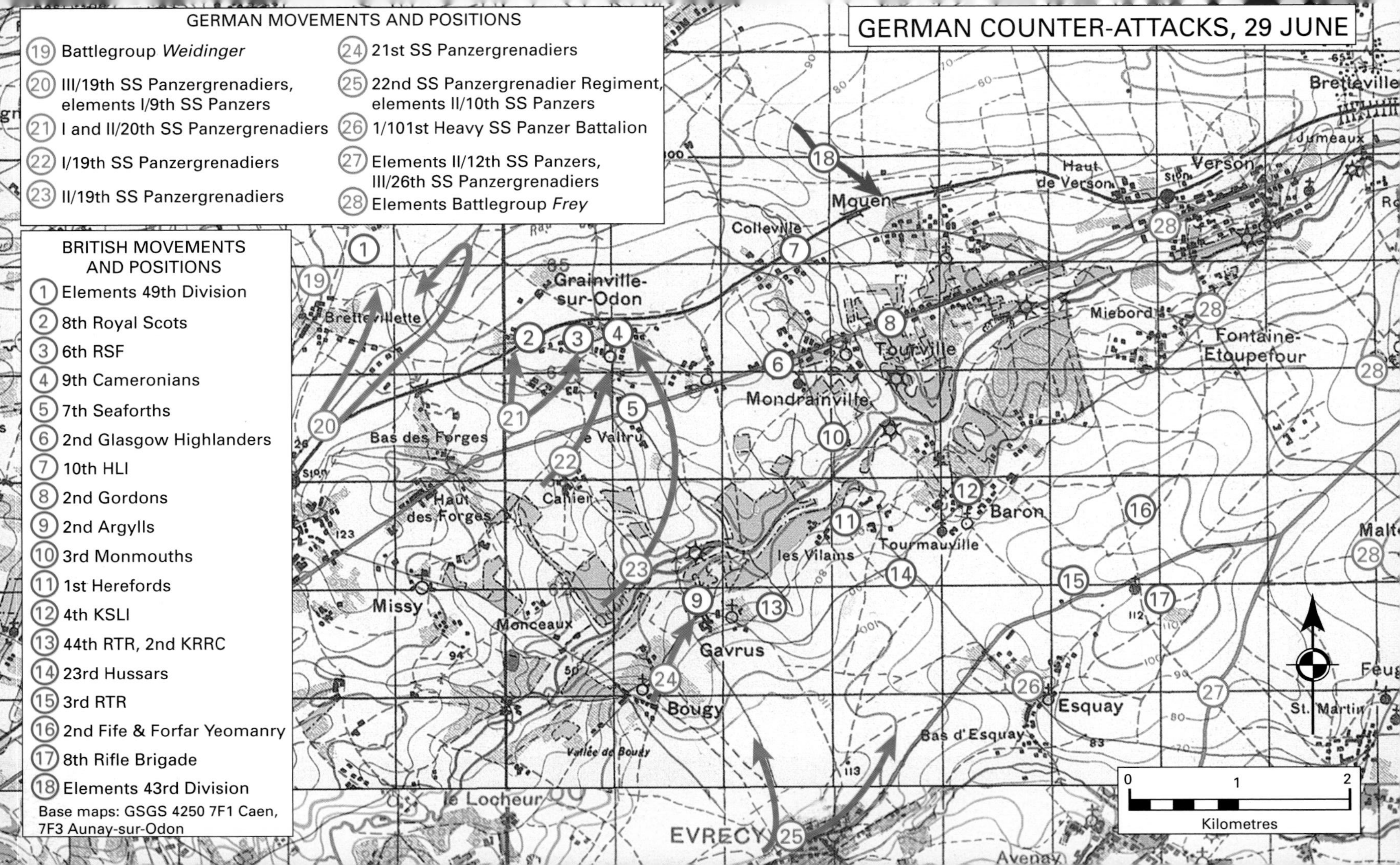
GERMAN COUNTER-ATTACKS, 29 JUNE
GERMAN MOVEMENTS AND POSITIONS
19 Battlegroup *Weidinger*
20 III/19th SS Panzergrenadiers, elements I/9th SS Panzers
21 I and II/20th SS Panzergrenadiers
22 I/19th SS Panzergrenadiers
23 II/19th SS Panzergrenadiers
24 21st SS Panzergrenadiers
25 22nd SS Panzergrenadier Regiment, elements II/10th SS Panzers
26 1/101st Heavy SS Panzer Battalion
27 Elements II/12th SS Panzers, III/26th SS Panzergrenadiers
28 Elements Battlegroup *Frey*
BRITISH MOVEMENTS AND POSITIONS
1 Elements 49th Division
2 8th Royal Scots
3 6th RSF
4 9th Cameronians
5 7th Seaforths
6 2nd Glasgow Highlanders
7 10th HLI
8 2nd Gordons
9 2nd Argylls
10 3rd Monmouths
11 1st Herefords
12 4th KSLI
13 44th RTR, 2nd KRRC
14 23rd Hussars
15 3rd RTR
16 2nd Fife & Forfar Yeomanry
17 8th Rifle Brigade
18 Elements 43rd Division
Base maps: GSGS 4250 7F1 Caen, 7F3 Aunay-sur-Odon
Bretteville
Jumeaux
Verson
Haut de Verson
Mouen
Colleville
Grainville-sur-Odon
Brettevillette
Tourville
Miebord
Fontaine-Etoupefour
Mondrainville
Bas des Forges
Haut des Forges
Cahier
Baron
Tourmauville
les Vilains
Missy
Monceaux
Gavrus
Bougy
Vallée de Bougy
Esquay
Bas d'Esquay
St. Martin
le Locheur
EVRECY
Avenay
Kilometres
0
1
2

Division and Battlegroup *Frey* were to exert some pressure on the eastern and south-eastern flank. The attacks were to have begun at 0700 hours on 29 June. That proved impossible, however, for Bittrich's corps, with almost 250 tanks and assault guns, was hit hard by the massive impact of Allied air power. Thus the German attack was postponed until the afternoon. (In addition to the summary given below further details on these attacks are given in Tour D, *pages 171–82.*)

9th SS Panzer Division, now led by *SS-Standartenführer* (Colonel) Thomas Müller, began its attack on the front Noyers-Bocage–Haut des Forges–Vendes shortly after 1400 hours. The division sought to cut right across the Scottish Corridor with Battlegroup *Weidinger* protecting its left flank. The division's main effort was by III/19th SS Panzergrenadiers, advancing along the Noyers-Bocage–Cheux road, supported by a company of Panthers from I/9th SS Panzers. They crossed the Rauray spur and then ran into the British defensive positions. Here they were hit by anti-tank and artillery fire and only achieved a salient between Grainville-sur-Odon and Rauray. 9th SS Panzer Division's main effort had failed.

Secondary attacks against Grainville-sur-Odon and le Valtru were made by I and II/19th SS Panzergrenadiers, later reinforced by part of 20th SS Panzergrenadiers; these made a little progress but were eventually repulsed. Thus, by dusk, the division was forced to withdraw back to its start line.

10th SS Panzer Division, commanded by *SS-Standartenführer* Heinz Harmel, was delayed in launching its counter-attack by attacks from Allied aircraft and therefore did not set off until 1430 hours. As a result of the clash between 44th RTR and Harmel's units earlier that morning, the British were ready and waiting. There were two thrusts by the German division, one towards Gavrus – the main effort – and the other towards Hills 113 and 112. 21st SS Panzergrenadier Regiment led the attack against Gavrus, supported by self-propelled guns of 7/ and 8/10th SS Panzer Regiment. They advanced from Bougy and broke into Gavrus to engage 2nd Argylls, having run into patrols from 8th Rifle Brigade. An intense fight developed in which 2nd Argylls was gradually pushed back to the southern bridge, but the Germans were unable to advance any further. Meanwhile, 21st SS Panzergrenadier Regiment attacked from Neuilly towards the Tourmauville bridge. Under heavy British artillery bombardment the Germans entered Évrecy and then fought for the rest of the day to establish themselves

The motorised infantry of 8th Rifle Brigade and the Shermans of 23rd Hussars in the vicinity of Hill 112 on 29 June. The nearest vehicle is an M5 half-tracked personnel carrier. The Odon valley is in the background. *(IWM B6193)*

on Hill 113. By the evening the Germans had taken the high ground, but the struggle to do so had lasted so long that the attack on Esquay-Notre-Dame and Hill 112 had to be postponed.

The fighting, however, had sapped the strength of those British units holding the line around Grainville-sur-Odon and later in the day the commander of 44th Brigade, Brigadier H.D.K. Money, began to reinforce the front. By dawn the next day 6th KOSB, plus a 17-pounder troop of 97th Anti-Tank Regiment that was under Money's command, had dug in on a line through the Grainville château, between the Noyers-Bocage road and the railway. 15th Division's reconnaissance regiment on the right created a link between 6th KOSB north of Grainville-sur-Odon and 49th Division in Rauray, with 8th Royal Scots and 6th RSF in depth behind, meaning that the British were able to maintain strong positions.

Meanwhile, Brigadier C.M. Barber's 46th Brigade was in good positions around le Valtru and Mondrainville and was further strengthened when 7th RTR, 10th HLI and 2nd Gordons came under command. The other battalion in Brigadier J.R. Mackintosh-Walker's 227th Brigade, 2nd Argylls, remained at Gavrus.

The British defended well against the counter-attacks of II SS Panzer Corps on the afternoon and evening of 29 June. The green British troops with their generally poorer equipment and weaponry were more than able to hold their own against their experienced and better-armed enemy. The success that 15th Division had in its battles on 29 June was down to the careful positioning of its defences – not least by using the *bocage* to its advantage – and excellent leadership and tactical prowess at the small unit level. Also critical to the failure of the German counter-attacks on that day, however, was the massive Allied accomplishment of battlefield air interdiction – the disruption of the Germans as they moved to assemble for their attacks. The continued threat from Bittrich's corps was enough, nevertheless, to stop any further British advances and to keep VIII Corps on a defensive footing. This change of tack during a major Allied offensive that had progressed just a few kilometres and yet was supposed to make Caen untenable was, to say the least, unfortunate.

49th Division troops digging in near Rauray on 29 June. The standard M4 Sherman tank seen here was armed with a 75-mm gun and two .30-calibre machine guns. *(IWM B6225)*

The failure of II SS Panzer Corps to make any great impact with its counter-attack was a great concern to Bittrich, who demanded that the attacks be restarted that same night in order to negate the impact of Allied air supremacy. Thus, in the few hours available to them, Müller and Harmel reorganised their divisions and made their plans to attack again. On the 9th SS Panzer Division front in the early hours of 30 June, there were renewed attacks in the area of Grainville-sur-Odon and le Valtru by 19th SS Panzergrenadier Regiment and on the left by 20th SS Panzergrenadier Regiment. Little headway was made, however, against a screen of reconnaissance Cromwells deployed by 2nd Northamptonshire Yeomanry, and heavy British artillery bombardments shattered the Germans' cohesion.

The area near Bougy where 10th SS Panzer Division formed up for the attack on Gavrus. *(Author)*

On the 10th SS Panzer Division front, the attack began at 0120 hours. 22nd SS Panzergrenadier Regiment and II/10th SS Panzer Regiment advanced to Avenay and then on to Vieux, in order to try to push on to Hill 112. During the night 21st SS Panzergrenadier Regiment also prepared for another attack on Gavrus. This was not launched until later in the morning, however, and was unsuccessful. An attack on Baron-sur-Odon also failed after accurate British artillery fire and a counter-attack. During this period, the fact that some British armour had been left behind when both 4th and 29th Armoured Brigades withdrew back across the

A knocked out 88-mm gun near Évrecy that seems to have seen extensive action considering the spent shell cases lying around. *(IWM B8666)*

Odon was critical in the defence of the bridgehead. It was clear to the German divisional commanders and Bittrich at II SS Panzer Corps that the chances of a major breakthrough against VIII Corps were slim, and so the counter-attacks were called off.

VIII Corps on 30 June

O'Connor's redeployment of 4th and 29th Armoured Brigades had begun in the last hour of 29 June and was completed at dawn on the following day. Although they did not know it, the British had weathered the worst of Bittrich's storm and yet were still battening down the hatches ready for an even more formidable strike that was never to come. 31st Tank Brigade was placed in support of the infantry while anti-tank guns were positioned in depth along the Scottish Corridor. 4th and 29th Armoured Brigades, meanwhile, were concentrated in positions around Norrey-en-Bessin so that they could be used to counter-attack against any German incursions into the British line. It was in these defensively-minded hours that Lt-Gen Dempsey decided to end Operation Epsom.

With both the British and German commanders having taken the decision not to launch any more major offensive movements on the Odon, one might be forgiven for thinking that a lull descended on the battlefield. This was, in fact, far from the truth, with both sides trying to consolidate their positions. The Germans did not take up a defensive posture and their infantry and armour continued to hit the British with a series of minor attacks launched on narrow fronts. Thus, during the late morning of 30 June, 10th SS Panzer Division probed at Gavrus and launched an attack on Hill 112 with units from 22nd SS Panzergrenadier Regiment, II/10th SS Panzers and, attacking from Maltot, II/12th SS Panzers. Supporting the attack were guns from the division but also from II SS Panzer Corps, 12th SS Panzer Division and 7th and 8th Projector Brigades. The result was that the already vacant Hill 112 fell once again to the Germans, at around noon. In mid-afternoon 9th SS Panzer Division also struck and, once again, it was in the Grainville–le Valtru area. Müller achieved some penetration of the southern positions before being ejected by 7th Seaforths.

Maj-Gen Roberts of 11th Armoured Division moving forward in a White M3A1 armoured scout car. *(IWM B9183)*

Assisted by the capture of Hills 112 and 113, the Germans shelled and mortared the battlefield ceaselessly. This made it extremely difficult for the British to move anything up or down the road from the Odon to Cheux and the Odon valley (or 'Death Valley' as it became known) became extremely dangerous. The British returned fire, however, with 43rd Division's 94th, 112th and 179th Field Regiments, RA, being extremely busy during this period. Also, 8th AGRA fired approximately 38,000 rounds in the reporting period 30 June – 1 July. During this time, casualties continued to be taken on both sides. For the British in particular, evacuating the wounded back to the safety of rear areas proved extremely difficult, considering the excellent observation that the Germans enjoyed from their lofty perches just south of the Odon.

VIII Corps staff officers examining a *Leibstandarte* tunic. In the foreground is Captain Hunt and to the rear is Major G.S. Jackson. *(IWM B6229)*

With movement on the north bank of the Odon hazardous, and with new attacks being mounted on Gavrus, Maj-Gen MacMillan decided on the afternoon of 30 June to withdraw 2nd Argylls. The battalion had remained isolated and had taken heavy casualties from its fight with 10th SS Panzer Division. 2nd Argylls was therefore pulled back to Colleville, where it found the headquarters of 227th Brigade. The Germans then moved forward to fill the military vacuum in the village. Meanwhile, 15th Division reorganised itself, with its brigades retaking control of their own assets and some of the battalions being moved once more. Nothing remained easy in the Odon valley, however, with the ground

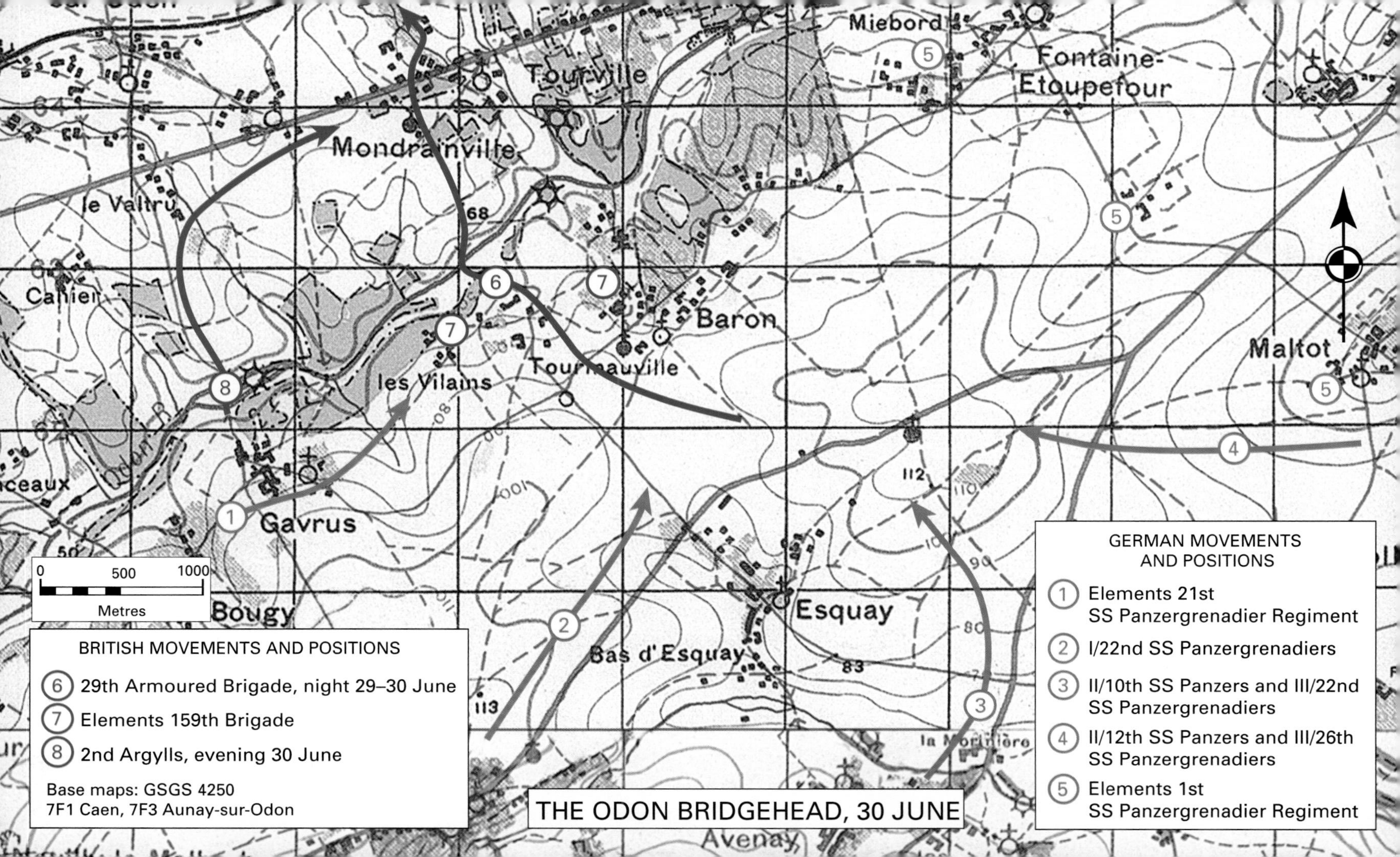

THE ODON BRIDGEHEAD, 30 JUNE

conditions extremely wet, the mosquitoes driving the troops mad and German bombardments frequent. It was, therefore, an extremely grateful 46th Brigade that was relieved that night by 160th Brigade of 53rd Division. 46th Brigade moved back to le Mesnil-Patry to rest and reorganise.

By the night of 30 June/1 July, the British had called a halt to Operation Epsom. Having prepared themselves for a full onslaught by II SS Panzer Corps, they found instead that the Germans pushed and probed in relatively minor ways on narrow fronts. Bittrich's troops did fill the gaps left by the withdrawing British, such as on Hill 112 and at Gavrus, but in spite of British preparations, there was no need for concern. As for the Germans themselves, II SS Panzer Corps was not in a position to launch anything more powerful and although its men sat atop Hills 112 and 113 and shelled the British in the Odon valley, there was little more that they could do. On the battlefield, Epsom ended, rather ignominiously, in a sort of draw.

30 June: Elements of 11th Armoured Division's 23rd Hussars make their way up the line. Note the churned up ground. *(IWM B6363)*

CHAPTER 5

AFTER OPERATION EPSOM

If 30 June saw a reassessment by both the British and the Germans of their short-term offensive options in the vicinity of the Odon, then early July saw both apply the conclusions to their deliberations. However, on 1 July both 9th and 10th SS Panzer Divisions launched renewed attacks towards their previously stated objectives both north and south of the Odon. The battlefield commanders wondered what their superiors thought that the corps could achieve against the continued might of VIII Corps. Hausser, for example, pointed out to Rommel that 'tenacious enemy resistance will prevent our counter-offensive from having any appreciable effect'. Bittrich also had severe misgivings about throwing his divisions against O'Connor's men but, unaware that Epsom had been halted, believed that he must do all that was possible to stop the British armour from exploiting south of the Odon.

Units of 10th SS Panzer Division, therefore, struck at 0430 hours from the south-west against the bridgehead held by 159th Brigade. Baron-sur-Odon was taken, but 31st Tank Brigade was rushed forward to counter-attack and the village was recaptured at around noon. 9th SS Panzer Division attacked at just after 0600 hours with Battlegroup *Weidinger*, once again, on its left. The attack slammed into 160th Brigade of 53rd Division in the area of le Valtru on the right, 44th Brigade in the vicinity of the Grainville château in the centre, and 70th Brigade of 49th Division on the left. It was in the centre and on the left that the pressure was heaviest and there was intense and confused fighting here for several hours. Nevertheless, the British did not give ground thanks to their substantial reinforcements, the application of some heavy and accurate artillery fire and then their successful counter-attacks. In response, the Germans withdrew.

These attacks therefore, failed once again and on 2 July II SS Panzer Corps was ordered to consolidate the ground that it had already taken. The German line now ran from Verson through Éterville to Hill 112, down to a point just short of Tourmauville and then on to the northern edge of Gavrus before continuing over the Odon to the west of le Valtru and up towards Brettevillette. The German counter-attacks therefore came to an end and for a period of over a week both sides prodded and probed the

The remarkable sight of camouflaged 31st Tank Brigade armour after Operation Epsom. *(IWM B7078)*

opposition's line in order to better their local tactical positions. On 2 July, for example, 12th SS Panzer Division attacked on both sides of the Caen–Villers-Bocage highway and managed to consolidate at Fontaine-Étoupefour.

Meanwhile, 15th Division was relieved by 53rd Division in the west of the corridor, while in the east 43rd Division continued to hold the line. Both divisions suffered from the excellent observation that the Germans still enjoyed from Hill 112, which continued to be a running sore for the British. As Hausser said, 'He who holds Hill 112 holds Normandy,' and there would be further bloody attempts to take it – but not yet. VIII Corps' focus was, therefore, like the Germans', to hold the positions that had already been won. This did not mean that the Allies had taken pressure off the Germans in Normandy, of course, just that VIII Corps was given a chance to rest and reorganise before being thrown into the fray once more. Thus, as O'Connor's officers endeavoured to learn the many valuable lessons that arose from their experiences in Epsom (which, inevitably, presented a steep learning curve for all concerned), the Allies began a new set of offensive operations. For the Americans, having finally taken Cherbourg on 29 June, the aim was to push towards south Brittany while for Second (British) Army, the focus remained on Caen. Operation 'Charnwood' succeeded in taking the city on 8–9 July. Operation 'Jupiter' was launched on 10 July in an attempt to tidy up the area to the west of Caen (including the capture of Hill 112) and then Operation 'Goodwood' began from the Orne bridgehead in the third week of July. There was no let up in the offensive action by the Allies. Epsom, at the very least, had played its part in weakening the German ability to defend Normandy.

A staff officer of VIII Corps plotting positions on a map in the Odon area on 2 July. He wears an armlet which, if blue and yellow, denotes that he is an officer of the Royal Artillery or Royal Engineers survey company. *(IWM B6292)*

3 July: the road out of Cheux. *(IWM B6321)*

To assess whether Operation Epsom was a success or not one might merely examine whether the offensive achieved its aims; the difficulty is, however, knowing exactly what those aims were. For while it is clear that the stated aims of Epsom – to cross the Orne and dominate the southern approaches to Caen – were not achieved, it could be argued that the unstated aims were. Some, including Montgomery himself, have argued that these unstated aims were the truly important objectives for they had strategic implications that far outweighed the capture of Bretteville-sur-Laize. Others, however, argue that the Montgomery's 'wider ambitions' were merely a fig leaf snatched by the Land Commander to cover up yet another embarrassing failure. The fig leaf was Montgomery's argument that, although Epsom failed to achieve its operational objectives, success was nevertheless attained as Caen fell a little more than a week after the offensive was ended. More importantly, Epsom further weakened the German hold on Normandy by sapping their strength. In this vein Montgomery went to great pains to ensure that all who were willing to listen knew that it was Second (British) Army which attracted the bulk of the German armour to it in Normandy and, of course, that Epsom broke II SS Panzer Corps' sword as it was being thrust towards Bayeux.

Troops from 11th Armoured Division holding a communion service shortly after Operation Epsom. *(IWM B6855)*

Why did Montgomery need to make such assertions and was what he said accurate? Montgomery's motives for banging the Second Army drum are obvious from a national perspective. As a British general himself, he wanted to ensure that the British Army was seen in the best possible light. However, when national pride was mixed with other political, military and personality-led motives, the brew became complex, murky and explosive. The constant grappling and griping within the Allies' higher command was as unsavoury as it was likely when one considers the pressures and the personalities involved. In such circumstances, and with responsibility for all land operations in Normandy, Montgomery wanted to ensure that the success of an army was not measured by the ground that it had taken. The Anglo-Canadian forces had struggled to make progress around Caen for very good reason, he said, not least because the terrain in the area was extremely difficult and the Germans were willing to defend it at all costs. Montgomery was correct – Second (British) Army was fighting over more difficult ground than the Americans, the German defences were stronger and included far more panzer divisions than were facing the Americans – but he still had to 'make progress'.

To a cautious and deep-thinking general like Montgomery, an 'attritional' campaign was necessary even if it was not what the politicians, his military superiors and the home front wanted or expected. However, Montgomery wanted short sharp jabs at the Germans with minimal casualties to his own troops rather than the rather unsavoury slogging matches that Field Marshal Douglas Haig had engaged in just over a quarter of a century earlier. As a result, Montgomery's operations in Normandy, such as Epsom, had stated operational aims, but also wider unstated strategic aims – fixing the enemy forces and destroying them. However, the problem with both Haig and Montgomery was that, because of the pressure that was on them, both men tended to exaggerate their chances of

German prisoners being escorted back across the Odon. *(IWM B7426)*

a breakthrough success rather than the importance of maintaining the initiative, wearing down the enemy and advancing in steps rather than in bounds. Thus, Epsom, touted as a 'blitz attack', was, ironically, more notable for its attritional value and its dislocation of the Germans in Normandy than it was for British manoeuvre.

A young *Waffen-SS* officer is questioned by an intelligence officer from VIII Corps. *(IWM B5973)*

The operation cost VIII Corps about 4,000 casualties and the Germans over 3,000, but while Allied troop numbers were still growing – VIII Corps was 22,735 men stronger on 30 June than it had been on 26 June – this was not true for their enemy. Thus, with his division having suffered 1,244 casualties as a result of Epsom, Kurt Meyer wrote, 'The 12th SS Panzer Division can no longer be considered fully operational. The remnants have, at best, the combat value of a weak battlegroup.' He was probably overstating his case, but 12th SS Panzer Division had been weakened by the operation,

The 15th Division memorial on the D89 road south of Tourville-sur-Odon. *(Author)*

not fatally, but certainly significantly. The same was true of II SS Panzer Corps and this led to Field Marshal Gerd von Rundstedt, German Commander-in-Chief West, writing in a situation report on 30 June that the Germans had suffered 'grievous losses' on the Odon. 9th SS Panzer Division had lost 1,145 men, six Panthers and

16 Panzer IV and 10 *Sturmgeschütze* armoured vehicles. By 7 July it had only 43 Panthers, 15 Mark IVs and 23 *Sturmgeschützen* in a combat-ready condition. Since arriving in Normandy, therefore, the division had lost 36 Panthers, 33 Panzer IVs and 17 *Sturmgeschützen*. 10th SS Panzer Division, meanwhile, lost 571 men and an unknown but 'significant' number of tanks and other vehicles in Epsom. Von Schweppenburg was so worried by the state of the corps at the end of Epsom that he and Rommel planned to withdraw it from the sector; Berlin would not sanction this and so it stayed in the front line.

Casualties

VIII Corps suffered a total of 4,020 casualties in Operation Epsom. According to its divisional history, *15th (Scottish) Division* suffered 2,331 casualties in the period 27 June – 2 July; 31 officers and 257 other ranks were killed, 91 officers and 1,547 other ranks were wounded and 8 officers and 786 other ranks reported missing: a total of 130 officers and 2,590 other ranks. The losses were equally divided between the three brigades. As an example of the battalions, 2nd Gordons lost five officers killed, a further eight officers wounded and 254 other rank casualties.

11th Armoured Division and *43rd Division* lost 1,256 between them. Killed in action in 11th Armoured Division were: 2nd Northamptonshire Yeomanry 38; 8th Rifle Brigade 36; 23rd Hussars 36; 4th KSLI 34; 3rd Monmouths 30; 2nd Fife and Forfar Yeomanry 27; 3rd RTR 15; 1st Herefords: 12; Royal Artillery: 29.

II SS Panzer Corps was, therefore weakened by Operation Epsom, as were 12th SS Panzer Division and the battlegroups supplied by 1st and 2nd SS Panzer Divisions to counter-attack. The question remains, however, as to whether, without the offensive, as Montgomery argues, Bittrich's corps would have hampered the Americans and damaged the campaign. There is no doubt that VIII Corps' push across the Odon did attract the attention of 9th and 10th SS Panzer Divisions. It should be remembered, however, that the Germans had still not made definite plans about how to use the two divisions. It is possible, for example, that they could have been used against Bayeux in the British sector. Given the presence of powerful US and British forces in this general area, it seems unlikely that such an offensive could have succeeded. Thus, it could be argued, Epsom managed to deflecting a thrust by II SS Panzer Corps that was likely to have been a relatively weak rapier lunge on the British flank, rather than a critical blow from a heavy sword into the American midriff. Strategically, therefore, Epsom was undoubtedly important, but not quite in the way that Montgomery went to great lengths to propound.

> **Montgomery also put an interesting 'spin' on the failure of Epsom operationally, putting great emphasis on the impact of the Great Storm.**
>
> 'In fairer conditions the build-up of formations and stores might have been kept to schedule... 8 Corps operations might have succeeded in taking Caen before the flower of the SS Panzer formations had become available in its defence.'
>
> *Source:* quoted in D'Este, *Decision in Normandy*, p. 245.

A British motorcyclist has abandoned his machine near Rauray and tries to find out what is happening up the lane. A dead German lies nearby. *(IWM B6161)*

The weather did undoubtedly have a major impact on the battle although, once again, not quite in the way that Montgomery said. The preparations for Epsom were not all that they might have been, that is true; delays to certain formations arriving in Normandy meant that they could not carry out all the pre-operation tasks they had been trained to do. As a result, divisions and units went into their first battle in a rushed fashion – but in warfare this is not that uncommon. Far more serious was the detrimental impact that the

A Tiger tank from 101st Heavy SS Panzer Battalion lies abandoned near Rauray on the Epsom battlefield. In the war diaries and post-operational reports, most British contacts with German armour were described as engagements with Tiger tanks. In reality just a small fraction of them were. *(IWM B6155)*

weather had on the ability to apply air power to the battle. On 19 June Montgomery had written to his friend General Simpson at the War Office, 'It will be a blitz attack supported by all available air power', but, throughout the battle, poor weather severely undermined the ability of the British to wring all possible benefit from Allied air superiority. When the aircraft could fly, however, such as on the morning of 29 June, their impact could be considerable, as II SS Panzer Corps found out to its cost. Air power was not a panacea to all VIII Corps' ills, however, as was revealed by the failure to destroy the dug-in tanks on Hill 112 on 28 June.

If lack of support from the air was an important factor in the failure of Epsom to achieve its operational aims, it was by no means the only one. It should also be noted that VIII Corps was largely composed of novice formations, which were fighting a skilful, well-supplied and highly motivated opposition in well-prepared defensive positions set in difficult *bocage* terrain. In such a situation even experienced troops using the most relevant doctrine would have struggled. In Epsom, green troops with some poor equipment found that, although much of their doctrine and training helped them with the basics, it shed little light on the detail.

Thus, in the words of one commentator:

'Outdated military philosophies and old-fashioned discipline born and nurtured on the parade ground, had been shown to be badly wanting.'

Source: Reynolds, *Steel Inferno*, p. 141.

Generals O'Connor, Dempsey and Montgomery on 16 July. *(IWM B7407)*

Such a start point was hardly conducive to Montgomery's desire for a fast-moving advance, and the plan only exacerbated the problems by failing to deal with the open left flank, assuming the rapid capture of the Rauray spur and giving the Germans every opportunity to slow VIII Corps' momentum on a small and congested battlefield with few usable roads.

There have been many occasions in military history when such obstacles have been overcome by boldness and success has ensued

A German PaK 40 (75-mm) anti-tank gun with its dead gunner lying next to it in a lane through Fontenay-le-Pesnel. A knocked-out Panther can be seen in the background on the right and, behind a tree, a Sherman. *(IWM B5939)*

– but this was not one of those occasions. In Epsom boldness was replaced by caution at the higher levels of command – the decision to go on the defensive on 29 June in preparation for the II SS Panzer Corps counter-attack, for example, was hardly a gesture of daring – and as a result, the attack quickly became bogged down in the Odon valley. Interestingly, the British seem to have excelled when called upon to take up a defensive posture, but even this has to be balanced by the absolute suitability of the ground to the creation of good defensive positions and, perhaps, the relative weakness of the German counter-attacks. Such factors should not detract, though, from the achievements of VIII Corps, which was blooded in Epsom and did well considering the challenging circumstances.

For the survivors of the battle there was some opportunity for relaxation. The entertainer George Formby is seen here performing for VIII Corps troops on 30 July. *(IWM B8265)*

Maj-Gen G.H. MacMillan's letter of 5 July to the Gordons' regimental HQ back in Scotland sums up the situation for the units involved:

'The battalion is out of the line and having a well earned rest. Our first introduction to battle has been a very hard test: we had a week of hell from the multiple mortars... The one thing we can say is the battalion did all they were told to do... the Jocks behaved in their usual grand way... '

Source: quoted in Wilfred Miles, *The Life of a Regiment*, p. 271.

In the final analysis Operation Epsom failed and there were many operational and tactical lessons for all involved to absorb during the following days and weeks. However, when seen as part of Montgomery's series of rapid and consecutive blows against the German Army in Normandy, the importance of Epsom becomes more apparent and there is little doubt that it did play a significant part in the Allies' eventual success in the region.

Tributes

There were tributes paid by many Allied leaders and commentators to the officers and men of the Scottish Division, but they are summed up pithily by Monty's personal contribution in a letter he wrote to the divisional commander on 2 July.

From the Commander-in-Chief, 21st Army Group:

'I would like to congratulate the 15th Division as a whole on the very fine performance put up during the past week's fighting. The Division went into battle for the first time in this war; but it fought with great gallantry and displayed a grand offensive spirit. Scotland can well feel proud of the 15th Scottish Division and the whole Division can be proud of itself. Please congratulate the Division from me and tell all officers and men that I am delighted at what they have done.'

B.L. Montgomery

PART THREE

BATTLEFIELD TOURS

GENERAL TOURING INFORMATION

Normandy is a thriving holiday area, with some beautiful countryside, excellent beaches and very attractive architecture (particularly in the case of religious buildings). It was also, of course, the scene of heavy fighting in 1944, and this has had a considerable impact on the tourist industry. To make the most of your trip, especially if you intend visiting non-battlefield sites, we strongly recommend you purchase one of the general Normandy guidebooks that are commonly available. These include: *Michelin Green Guide: Normandy*; *Thomas Cook Travellers: Normandy*; *The Rough Guide to Brittany and Normandy*; *Lonely Planet: Normandy*.

TRAVEL REQUIREMENTS

First, make sure you have the proper documentation to enter France as a tourist. Citizens of European Union countries, including Great Britain, should not usually require visas, but will need to carry and show their passports. Others should check with the French Embassy in their own country before travelling. British citizens should also fill in and take Form E111 (available from main post offices), which deals with entitlement to medical treatment, and all should consider taking out comprehensive travel insurance. France is part of the Eurozone, and you should also check exchange rates before travelling.

GETTING THERE

The most direct routes from the UK to Lower Normandy are by ferry from Portsmouth to Ouistreham (near Caen), and from Portsmouth or Poole to Cherbourg. Depending on which you choose, and whether you travel by day or night, the crossing takes between four and seven hours. Alternatively, you can sail to Le Havre, Boulogne or Calais and drive the rest of the way. (Travel time from Calais to Caen is about four hours; motorway and bridge tolls may be payable depending on the exact route taken.) Another option is to use the Channel Tunnel. Whichever way you decide to travel, early booking is advised, especially during the summer months.

Above: The church at Norrey-en-Bessin, which had to be rebuilt after the Battle of Normandy. *(Author)*

Page 115: A Sherman tank at Rauray on 28 June. The '50' painted on the turret denotes that the tank is from the headquarters of 8th Armoured Brigade. *(IWM B6130)*

Although you can of course hire motor vehicles in Normandy, the majority of visitors from the UK or other EU countries will probably take their own. If you do so, you will also need to take: a full driving licence; your vehicle registration document; a certificate of motor insurance valid in France (your insurer will advise on this); spare headlight and indicator bulbs; headlight beam adjusters or tape; a warning triangle; and a sticker or number plate identifying which country the vehicle is registered in. Visitors from elsewhere should consult a motoring organisation in their home country for details of the documents and other items they will require.

Normandy's road system is well developed, although there are still a few choke points, especially around the larger towns during rush hour and in the holiday season. As a general guide, in clear conditions it is possible to drive from Cherbourg to Caen in less than two hours.

3rd County of London Yeomanry troopers mending damaged tracks to make fit again for battle. *(IWM B6330)*

The orchard on Hill 112, taken from the memorial. Hill 112 was the scene of some of the bitterest fighting of Operation Epsom. *(Author)*

ACCOMMODATION

Accommodation in Normandy is plentiful and diverse, from cheap campsites to five star hotels in glorious châteaux. However, early booking is advised if you wish to travel between June and August. The Epsom battlefield is quiet countryside; for local accommodation (and for such other facilities as restaurants and museums) one should look to either Bayeux or Caen. Useful contacts include:

French Travel Centre, 178 Piccadilly, London W1V 0AL; tel: 0870 830 2000; web: www.raileurope.co.uk

French Tourist Authority, 444 Madison Avenue, New York, NY 10022 (other offices in Chicago, Los Angeles and Miami); web: www.francetourism.com

Calvados Tourisme, Place du Canada, 14000 Caen; tel: +33 (0)2 31 86 53 30; web: www.calvados-tourisme.com

Office de Tourisme Intercommunal de Bayeux, Pont Saint-Jean, 14400 Bayeux; tel: +33 (0)2 31 51 28 28; web: www.bayeux-tourism.com

Maison du Tourisme de Cherbourg et du Haut-Cotentin, 2 Quai Alexandre III, 50100 Cherbourg-Octeville; tel: +33 (0)2 33 93 52 02; web: www.ot-cherbourg-cotentin.fr

Gîtes de France, La Maison des Gîtes de France et du Tourisme Vert, 59 Rue Saint-Lazare, 75 439 Paris Cedex 09; tel: +33 (0)1 49 70 75 75; web: www.gites-de-france.fr

BATTLEFIELD TOURING

Each volume in the 'Battle Zone Normandy' series contains three or more battlefield tours. These are intended to last from a few hours to a full day apiece. Some are best undertaken using motor transport, others should be done on foot, and many involve a mixture of the two. Owing to its excellent infrastructure and relatively gentle topography, Normandy also makes a good location for a cycling holiday; indeed, some of our tours are ideally suited to this method.

A 4th Armoured Brigade Daimler 'Dingo' scout car being camouflaged in the corner of a wood near Cheux at the end of 26 June. *(IWM B5969)*

In every case the tour author has visited the area concerned recently, so the information presented should be accurate and reasonably up to date. Nevertheless land use, infrastructure and rights of way can change, sometimes at short notice. If you encounter difficulties in following any tour, we would very much like to hear about it, so we can incorporate changes in future editions. Your comments should be sent to the publisher at the address provided at the front of this book.

To derive maximum value and enjoyment from the tours, we suggest you equip yourself with the following items:

- Appropriate maps. European road atlases can be purchased from a wide range of locations outside France. However, for navigation within Normandy, the French Institut Géographique National (IGN) produces maps at a variety of scales (www.ign.fr). The 1:100,000 series ('Top 100') is particularly useful when driving over larger distances; sheet 06 (Caen – Cherbourg) covers most of the invasion area. For pinpointing locations precisely, the current IGN 1:25,000 Série Bleue is best (extracts from this series are used for the tour maps in this book). These can be purchased in many places across Normandy. They can also be ordered in the UK from some bookshops, or from specialist dealers such as the Hereford Map Centre, 24–25 Church Street, Hereford HR1 2LR; tel: 01432 266322; web: <www.themapcentre.com>. Allow at least a fortnight's notice, although some maps may be in stock. The main Série Bleue sheets required to cover the areas discussed in this book are: 1512OT Bayeux and 1513E Thury-Harcourt, but some parts of the fighting also occurred in the areas covered by the adjoining 1513O Aunay-sur-Odon/Villers-Bocage and 1612OT Caen maps.
- Lightweight waterproof clothing and robust footwear are essential, especially for touring in the countryside.
- Take a compass, provided you know how to use one!
- A camera and spare films/memory cards.
- A notebook to record what you have photographed.
- A French dictionary and/or phrasebook. (English is widely spoken in the coastal area, but is much less common inland.)
- Food and drink. Although you are never very far in Normandy from a shop, restaurant or *tabac*, many of the tours do not pass directly by such facilities. It is therefore sensible to take some light refreshment with you.
- Binoculars. Most officers and some other ranks carried binoculars in 1944. Taking a pair adds a surprising amount of verisimilitude to the touring experience.

SOME DO'S AND DON'TS

Battlefield touring can be an extremely interesting and even emotional experience, especially if you have read something about the battles beforehand. In addition, it is fair to say that residents of Normandy are used to visitors, among them battlefield tourers, and generally will do their best to help if you encounter problems.

However, many of the tours in the 'Battle Zone Normandy' series are off the beaten track, and you can expect some puzzled looks from the locals, especially inland. In all cases we have tried to ensure that tours are on public land, or viewable from public rights of way. However, in the unlikely event that you are asked to leave a site, do so immediately and by the most direct route.

Prime Minister Winston Churchill and General B.L. Montgomery pictured with British senior officers on 22 July. *From left:* Lt-Gen G.C. Bucknall, XXX Corps; Lt-Gen N.M. Ritchie, XII Corps; Lt-Gen R. O'Connor, VIII Corps; Lt-Gen M. Dempsey, Second (British) Army; Lt-Gen J. Crocker, I Corps; Lt-Gen G. Simonds, II Canadian Corps; and Brigadier M.S. Chilton, Chief of Staff of Second (British) Army. *(IWM B7883)*

In addition: **Never remove 'souvenirs' from the battlefields.** Even today it is not unknown for farmers to turn up relics of the 1944 fighting. Taking these without permission may not only be illegal, but can be extremely dangerous. It also ruins the site for genuine battlefield archaeologists. Anyone returning from France should also remember customs regulations on the import of weapons and ammunition of any kind.

Be especially careful when investigating fortifications. Some of the more frequently-visited sites are well preserved, and several of them have excellent museums. However, both along the coast and inland there are numerous positions that have been left to decay, and which carry risks for the unwary. In particular, remember that

Infantry march past a burnt-out Sherman tank at Fontenay-le-Pesnel with a destroyed Panther just beyond on the other side of the road. *(IWM B6042)*

many of these places were the scenes of heavy fighting or subsequent demolitions, which may have caused severe (and sometimes invisible) structural damage. Coastal erosion has also undermined the foundations of a number of shoreline defences. Under no circumstances should underground bunkers, chambers and tunnels be entered, and care should always be taken when examining above-ground structures. If in any doubt, stay away.

Beware of hunting (shooting) areas (signposted *Chasse Gardée*). Do not enter these, even if they offer a short cut to your destination. Similarly, Normandy contains a number of restricted areas (military facilities and wildlife reserves), which should be avoided. Watch out, too, for temporary footpath closures, especially along sections of coastal cliffs.

If using a motor vehicle, keep your eyes on the road. There are many places to park, even on minor routes, and it is always better to turn round and retrace your path than to cause an accident. In rural areas avoid blocking entrances and driving along farm tracks; again, it is better to walk a few hundred metres than to cause damage and offence.

The Epsom Battlefield Then and Now

The Epsom battlefield has changed little since 1944, although new building and roads have altered certain areas. At the northern end, the open fields south of the start line at le Mesnil-Patry and Norrey-en-Bessin remain undeveloped. The line of villages that were the first objectives for 15th Division (St-Manvieu-Norrey–la Gaule–Cheux–le Haut du Bosq) have merged to form one long line of farms and houses, however. Orchards and strong stone farms still abound on the battlefield and continue to look like mini-fortresses. Up on the high ground on the British right flank, the villages of Rauray and Brettevillette have grown, but the view over the northern part of the battlefield has not been hindered by this and the British start line can be clearly seen. The railway line to the north of Grainville-sur-Odon and Mouen has been replaced by a fast highway, but the *bocage* remains intact and increases in density as the steep Odon valley is reached.

The Odon itself is not very deep or wide, but the surrounding countryside is marshy and its banks are densely wooded and steep. On the southern side of the river, the valley leads up to Hill 112 and its slopes in every direction are largely free from hedges and give way to large and open fields. The observation from the top of the hill is remarkable, with views down to Esquay-Notre-Dame, across to Hill 113, down into the Odon valley and across the entire southern area of the battlefield up to the Caen–Villers-Bocage road. Carpiquet airfield and Caen can also be seen on a clear day.

It takes just minutes to drive the length and breadth of the Operation Epsom battlefield today and this is striking considering how many troops and vehicles crowded into it in June 1944. What is also noticeable is the undulating nature of the terrain, the views that extend across the battlefield from the various pieces of high ground, the density of the *bocage*, the steepness of the Odon valley and, perhaps above all, why Hill 112 was such a prize.

Tourers may wish to pay their respects at some of the war cemeteries where the dead of the battles discussed in this book have been laid to rest. Most of the Operation Martlet casualties have been buried in Fontenay-le-Pesnel Commonwealth War Graves Commission Cemetery (south-east of Fontenay, a few hundred metres east of the D139 road). There are 520 graves here (457 British, 4 Canadian and 59 German). The Epsom dead are mostly in St-Manvieu-Norrey Cemetery (1 km west of St-Manvieu, just west of the junction of the D9 and D183 roads). St-Manvieu holds 2,183 graves: 1,623 British, 3 Canadian, 1 Australian and 556 German. Both cemeteries can be found on the map on page 127, though only Fontenay is identified as 'Cim Milit'.

Directions for the start of each tour are based on the assumption that tourers will begin on either the main Caen–Bayeux highway, the N13, or the Caen southern ring-road, the N814.

The strong stone buildings of le Haut du Bosq. *(Author)*

TOUR A

26 JUNE – THE FIRST OBJECTIVES

OBJECTIVE: A tour exploring the line of villages that were 15th Division's first objectives, ending on the high ground at Rauray.

DURATION/SUITABILITY: Half a day if in a car. Suitable for cyclists and the disabled.

Stand A1: Norrey-en-Bessin

DIRECTIONS: From the N13 Caen-Bayeux highway take the D83 to Norrey-en-Bessin. Follow the road towards Norrey-en-Bessin and take the right turn, the D172, into the centre of the village and park outside the church. There is a memorial here to 6th Canadian Armoured Regiment (1st Hussars) and The Regina Rifles Regiment of 3rd Canadian Infantry Division, which liberated the village.

THE ACTION: During the night of 24/25 June, the British artillery moved forward and guns were concealed in barns, orchards and woods just behind Norrey-en-Bessin and in the area of Bretteville-l'Orgueilleuse (on the other side of the N13). Meanwhile, the armour, infantry and supporting arms all also moved forward from the rear to their forward assembly areas just behind the Epsom start line, which ran through the village. The village itself was in British hands but, as it was in ruins with debris-strewn streets, it had been used as an outpost zone for observation until just before the attack. The armour was to start from behind the village (actually on the railway line between the village and the N13 road) and then advance on either side of Norrey-en-Bessin, but the infantry units found places which best suited their purpose forward of the armoured positions from which to launch their attacks. The armour was drawn from 31st Tank Brigade, with 9th RTR in this area, together with a number of 79th Armoured Division's 'funnies'. The funnies – flail tanks for making passages through minefields and one squadron equipped with Armoured Vehicles Royal Engineers (AVREs), which were used to overcome obstacles – were divided between 15th (Scottish) Division's two infantry brigades. 44th Brigade attacked in this area, with 6th RSF

Norrey-en-Bessin Canadian memorial. *(Author)*

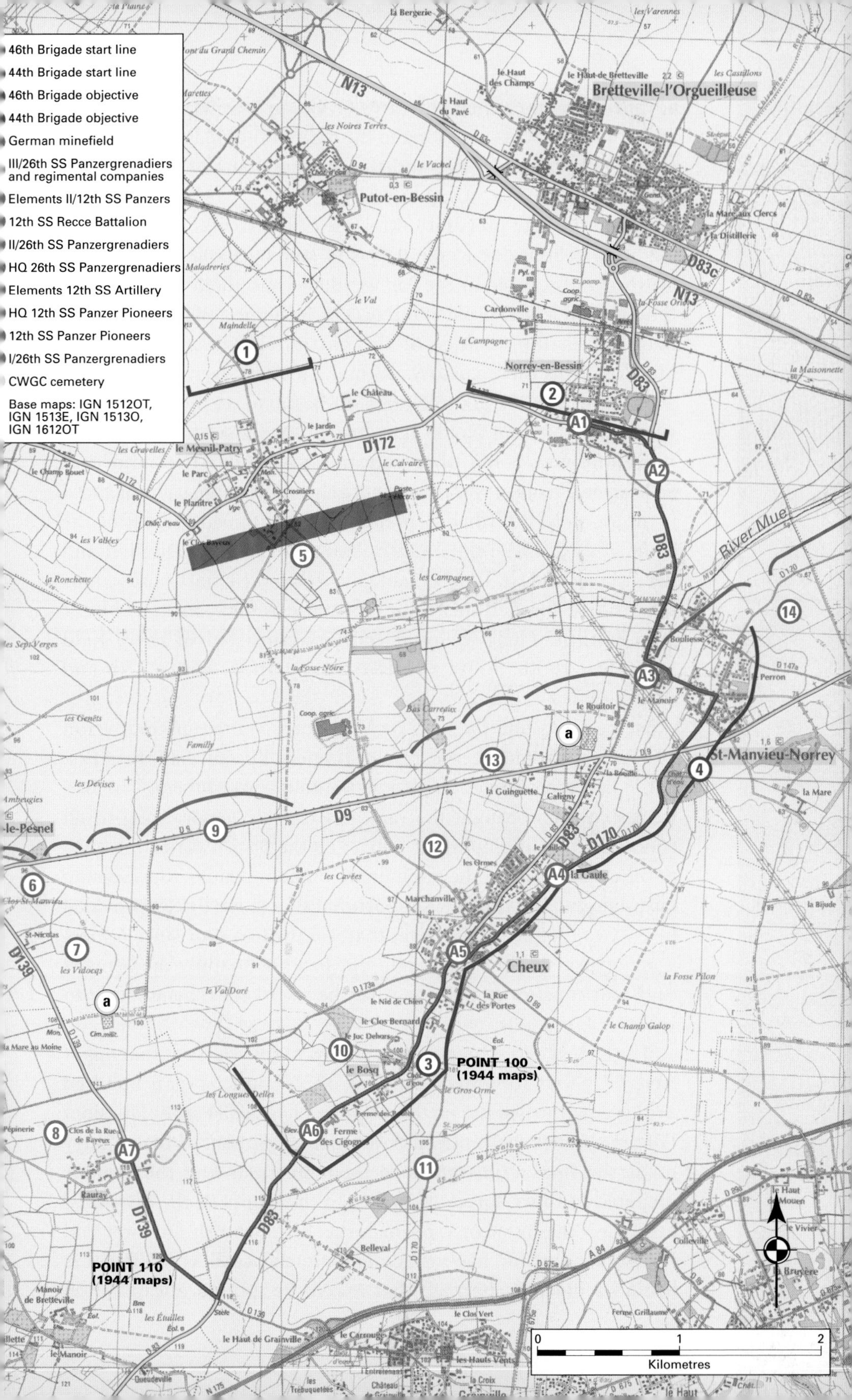
46th Brigade start line
44th Brigade start line
46th Brigade objective
44th Brigade objective
German minefield
III/26th SS Panzergrenadiers and regimental companies
Elements II/12th SS Panzers
12th SS Recce Battalion
II/26th SS Panzergrenadiers
HQ 26th SS Panzergrenadiers
Elements 12th SS Artillery
HQ 12th SS Panzer Pioneers
12th SS Panzer Pioneers
I/26th SS Panzergrenadiers
CWGC cemetery
Base maps: IGN 1512OT, IGN 1513E, IGN 1513O, IGN 1612OT
Bretteville-l'Orgueilleuse
Putot-en-Bessin
Norrey-en-Bessin
le Mesnil-Patry
St-Manvieu-Norrey
Cheux
River Mue
POINT 100 (1944 maps)
POINT 110 (1944 maps)
Kilometres

advancing to the east/left of Norrey-en-Bessin to St-Manvieu-Norrey and 8th Royal Scots attacking to the right of the village to la Gaule. 6th KOSB was in reserve and the machine guns of A Company, 1st Middlesex, were in support.

The immediate preparation for the offensive was not all that it might have been due to the delays in landing some of the troops in Normandy caused by the bad weather. Thus, there was little time for commanders to provide full orders, let alone conduct a full and detailed reconnaissance of the battlefield. Reconnaissance, therefore, was often cursory. To make matters even worse, when teams from 6th RSF got to Norrey-en-Bessin to see the ground over which the battalion would have to advance, they found that the front line was being observed and was under fire, and that St-Manvieu-Norrey was almost entirely hidden from sight in a fold in the ground. Nevertheless, preparations continued and during the night of 25/26 June the infantry battalions of 15th Division and the armour of 31st Tank Brigade moved to their start positions as the artillery finished their gun pits and carefully stockpiled their ammunition. The divisional artillery consisted of three field regiments, 190th, 131st and 181st, supporting 46th, 227th and 44th Brigades.

In the front line the men of VIII Corps waited anxiously for, although they had been carefully trained, Epsom was their first battle and their nerves jangled as the rain soaked them. The bad weather which brought the rain and was so demoralising to all concerned had an important impact on the British plans, for it led to the cancellation of the preliminary bombing raid on the German positions and the close air support that was to have been provided by 83 Group, RAF. This meant that, for the first time since 6 June, a major British offensive would not be able to apply the benefits of the air superiority that the Allies had worked so assiduously to achieve.

The lack of aerial support was a blow to the plan, but that might have been was forgotten when, at 0720 hours, several hundred British guns opened fire on the outposts of 12th SS Panzer Division. For ten minutes shells rained down on the Germans as the infantry made the final adjustments to their positions and the armour prepared to move forward. It was, in the words of the divisional historian, 'the moment for which the 15th Scottish Division had been preparing for five years'. The attack began at 0730 hours behind a creeping barrage that raked the ground ahead of the

A view looking north across the D9 over St-Manvieu-Norrey to Norrey-en-Bessin. The church can just be seen in the distance. *(Author)*

infantry, moving forward at a rate of 100 metres every three minutes. It was critical for the infantry and tanks to keep up with the barrage, staying between 500 and 1,000 metres behind, in order to attain the greatest benefit from it, as any sort of gap would allow the sheltering Germans time in which to return to their defensive positions. In order for this critical artillery support to work, there was close co-operation between the infantry battalions and the field regiments, with a forward observation officer and an OP party attached to each company and advancing with it. The barrage was earsplitting for anyone in the vicinity and an impressive sight for the infantry as they moved off.

Lieutenant Robert Woollcombe of 6th KOSB later wrote:

'It was like rolls of thunder, only it never seemed to slacken… Hurling itself onto strongpoints, enemy gun areas, forming up places, tank laagers, and above all concentrated into the creeping mass of shells that raked ahead of our infantrymen, as thousands of gunners bent to their tasks.'

Source: quoted in Tim Saunders, *Operation Epsom*, p. 40.

Men of No. 12 Platoon, B Company, 6th RSF, just moments before they attacked from Norrey-en-Bessin on 26 June. *(IWM B5950)*

The Royal Artillery seem to have done an extremely good job, for the commander of 12th SS Panzer Division, *SS-Standartenführer* Kurt Meyer, later wrote, 'The earth seemed to open up and gobble us all up. All hell had been let loose.' This was the beginning of the 'blitz' that Montgomery had talked about.

Stand A2: The 6th RSF sunken lane

DIRECTIONS: Return to the D83 and turn right. Pull in on to a cart track on the left after 100 metres.

The area over which 6th RSF attacked towards St-Manvieu-Norrey from the sunken lane which was the attack's starting point. *(Author)*

THE ACTION: This sunken lane was chosen as the springboard for the 6th RSF attack in an attempt to get the battalion as close to the creeping barrage as possible. All such decisions were compromises, with the brigade commander and commanding officer (Lt-Col J.G. Shillington) both hoping that the advanced position, just 125 metres from the opening barrage line, would save lives in the long run due to the surprise of their attack, even though there was always the possibility of the waiting troops being hit by 'shorts' from their own artillery. It should be remembered that worn gun barrels, poor gun calibration and faulty ammunition could all cause shells to fall in front of their target, and when so many guns were in use it was impossible to tell which was the rogue gun and silence it. The men of 6th RSF did suffer some casualties as a result of 'friendly fire' as they crouched in this lane. Two of the B Squadron, 9th RTR, tanks supporting the battalion then fell victim to anti-tank mines just forward of the start line, probably laid by the Canadians earlier in the month when they held this sector.

Even so, in spite of these minor difficulties, 6th RSF and the armour moved forward through the mist and into the large open cornfields containing the German outpost zone and leading to St-Manvieu-Norrey. As soon as the attack began, advanced German mortar and artillery shells, directed from observers of 12th SS Panzer Artillery Regiment in the vicinity of Carpiquet airfield, plunged towards the battalion and more casualties were sustained. For these green troops, disorientation and confusion in these circumstances were inevitable, but generally the battalion kept its direction well. Camouflaged riflemen (not snipers as many believed) who had survived the barrage sought further to confuse the situation, however. The advance was slow and it took the battalion an hour to advance the kilometre to St-Manvieu-Norrey.

The ruined church of St-Manvieu-Norrey. *(Author)*

Stand A3: St-Manvieu-Norrey

DIRECTIONS: Continue south along the D83 and follow the road down to the River Mue (a stream). As 6th RSF crossed the Mue at this point, it began to take significant casualties. Take the second road on the left and enter the village of St-Manvieu-Norrey (formerly St-Mauvieu). Stop at the ruined church, which was never

A view across the Mue valley from the D83 towards St-Manvieu-Norrey. It was across this ground that 6th RSF approached the village. *(Author)*

rebuilt after the fighting here in June 1944 and stands as a stark reminder to the ferocity of the battle in this area on 26–27 June.

THE ACTION: The village of St-Manvieu-Norrey was stoutly defended on 26 June by I/26th SS Panzergrenadiers, which poured fire into the advancing 6th RSF as the British battalion approached the village at 0830 hours. Just breaking into the German positions proved difficult. It took some accurate British bombardments, together with the firepower of the demolition guns mounted on AVREs of 81st Squadron, 6th Assault Regiment, RE, and the armour of 9th RTR, to achieve breaches in the defences at 0940 hours. The German positions in the village were strong, mutually supporting, and made excellent use of the stout buildings in the centre and the farmhouses, orchards and hedgerows on the periphery. Crocodile tanks were called forward to flame certain buildings and strongpoints, including the headquarters of I/26th SS Panzergrenadiers, which was eventually flamed by 141st (Buffs) Regiment, RAC, but several tanks were lost to *Panzerfausts*. The Germans were slowly overrun, but few surrendered and there was some bloody hand-to-hand fighting in and around the buildings before the village was brought under control at 1030 hours. Even then some confused actions continued in the village for the rest of the day.

The German counter-attacks that took place against St-Manvieu-Norrey that evening were conducted by a company of 21st Panzer Division tanks and some infantry from 25th SS Panzergrenadier Regiment. 6th RSF managed to beat them back, however, using machine-gun fire and, critically, the accurate artillery fire provided by 181st Field Regiment, RA. Nevertheless, recognising that St-Manvieu-Norrey was under threat, the commander of 44th Brigade, Brigadier Money, sent his reserve battalion – 6th KOSB (less one company that was ordered to reinforce 8th Royal Scots in la Gaule) – to relieve 6th RSF. 6th KOSB arrived in the village at around 1800 hours and within a couple of hours found itself beating off another counter-attack.

The orchards of la Gaule, so typical of the Normandy countryside. *(Author)*

Stand A4: La Gaule

DIRECTIONS: Continue to the crossroads with the new church and turn right on to the D170 signed to Cheux. La Gaule, Cheux and le Haut du Bosq have all merged since 1944 to become one enlarged Cheux. Continue across the crossroads with the D9 and, if possible to do so safely, stop and look back at Norrey-en-Bessin

26 June: Tanks of A Squadron, 9th RTR, advance south from the damaged church and village of Norrey-en-Bessin. *(IWM B6054)*

in order to attain a true perspective of what the Germans saw of the 44th Brigade attack. Continue down the D170, which has orchards on either side. Drive carefully – there are very few places to pull over – and if possible pull over on the track to the left leading down to some houses. There is not much to see in la Gaule

today. The sturdy farmhouses remain, but there is no village centre as such, although a short walk is always useful in obtaining views and spotting important ground that cannot be seen from a car.

THE ACTION: La Gaule was the objective of 44th Brigade's 8th Royal Scots and A Squadron, 9th RTR. Similarly disorientated and disrupted by the German defensive fire, hidden riflemen, the smoke and the mist, the British armour and infantry tried their utmost to keep up with the barrage and consequently fell on some German outpost positions before the enemy knew what was happening. One prisoner later said that he and some colleagues had taken cover from the barrage and then 'emerged only to find ourselves surrounded by tanks or furious Scotsmen throwing grenades.' Nevertheless, like 6th RSF on its left, 8th Royal Scots was slowed by the weight of the German fire and the distance between the battalion and the exploding shells of the supporting barrage grew alarmingly fast. Thus, by the time that 8th Royal Scots crossed the Caen–Fontenay-le-Pesnel road, about 1 km to the north of the village, it was already 0930 hours. It had taken the battalion two hours to advance 2.5 km. The tanks and infantry reached la Gaule at 1000 hours and managed to enter and clear the village quickly before digging in. The speed with which they took the village itself was undoubtedly due to the fact that they attacked on the boundary between I/26th SS Panzergrenadiers in St-Manvieu-Norrey and 12th SS Panzer Pioneer Battalion, defending Cheux. The village continued to be shelled and mortared throughout the day and a number of minor German counter-attacks were mounted, but all were repelled. 5th Wiltshires from 43rd Division relieved 8th Royal Scots during the night.

Stand A5: Cheux

DIRECTIONS: Continue down the D170 and turn right on the first substantial road (Rue du Tripot). Drive along this road to a crossroads and turn left on to the D83 and park. This is the centre of Cheux and a bar-tabac-brasserie *Au Pierrot Bleu* can be seen. You can explore Cheux from this point and, if you wish, walk or drive back to the crossroads, turn left on the Rue de Marchanville and leave the village. On reaching the high ground, just before the junction with the D9, look northwards to Norrey-en-Bessin and le Mesnil-Patry. It was along this road that so much of VIII Corps passed before entering this critical village at the centre of the battlefield.

THE ACTION: As 44th Brigade was fighting for St-Manvieu-Norrey and la Gaule, 46th Brigade was closing in on its more distant objectives over to the right. 2nd Glasgow Highlanders, supported by B Squadron, 7th RTR, advanced to Cheux, which was defended by 12th SS Panzer Pioneer Battalion. Meanwhile 9th Cameronians and C Squadron, 7th RTR attacked le Haut du Bosq, which was defended by elements of 26th SS Panzergrenadiers. Just like its sister brigade, 46th Brigade struggled with the conditions as it moved through the open cornfields. To make matters worse, less than 1 km from the start line at le Mesnil-Patry, 2nd Glasgow Highlanders and its supporting armour ran into an anti-tank minefield that had been expertly laid by the German pioneers. The infantry continued their attack, but, as was the German intention, the supporting armour came to a halt while the flail tanks of B Squadron, 22nd Dragoons, (from 30th Armoured Brigade of 79th Armoured Division) beat a path through at 2.5 km per hour.

During this hiatus, the German mortars, artillery, anti-tank weapons and machine guns, together with the riflemen who had survived the barrage, caused considerable casualties (one forward

Central Cheux looking west. This village was in ruins by the time that the infantry of 15th Division reached it on 26 June. *(Author)*

company of 9th Cameronians lost all but one officer during this period). With the Germans having successfully separated the tanks from the infantry, the foot soldiers advanced alone, as the barrage rolled onwards (it only stopped briefly on the D9 Caen–Fontenay-le-Pesnel road), and a large gap opened up between the armour and the 2nd Glasgow Highlanders.

At this point it became clear that the distance between the brigade's start line and its objectives, some 3.5 km to Cheux and 5 km to le Haut du Bosq, was going to have a great impact on the troops' ability to stay up with the barrage and to use surprise to take the villages quickly. The mist helped the British infantry as they pushed forward, but with a lack of air cover, a barrage that was rolling too far ahead of them and armour that had been stalled by a minefield, they were incredibly vulnerable.

46th Brigade continued its advance, often finding that German riflemen who had survived the barrage in their deep and well-concealed positions appeared behind the leading troops, which further fragmented the infantry assault. Some of these German troops continued to fight *in situ* for three days before being overrun; others made their way back through the British to friendly lines at night. With its supporting tanks having caught up again, 2nd Glasgow Highlanders made its way through the German main line of resistance and came across the headquarters of 12th SS Panzer

Pioneer Battalion, which was on a small hill immediately south of the Caen to Fontenay-le-Pesnel road, just under a kilometre west of la Gaule.

> **The last report to divisional headquarters, sent by the German battalion commander at 0900 hours by telephone, ended abruptly:**
>
> 'Enemy artillery have destroyed any anti-tank defences. The battalion is being overrun by British tanks. Individual positions are still holding out around Cheux. Enemy tanks are trying to crush my dug-out. Where are our tanks? I need a counter-attack from the direction of the Rau... '
>
> *Source:* quoted in Tim Saunders, *Operation Epsom*, p. 53.

The German commander and staff then fought their way out of the position and, at around midnight, made their way back to their own lines. Meanwhile, 2nd Glasgow Highlanders and 7th RTR attacked Cheux, which was defended by a battery of 12th SS Panzer Artillery and supply platoons of 12th SS Panzer Pioneer Battalion acting as infantry. Cheux was a critical village as several roads converged on it from the north and then fanned out from it to the south. To take the village swiftly would greatly assist the momentum of the entire attack, but the Germans had, of course, noted its importance. The battle for Cheux was, therefore, intense with its defence led by two staff officers, *SS-Untersturmführer* (2nd Lt) Bruno Asmus, a technical officer, and *SS-Untersturmführer* Lorenz, a supply officer. Although lacking resources and, perhaps, the experience to conduct sophisticated defensive operations, these two men did a first-class job in putting yet another obstacle in the way of the British. Thus, Cheux had to be cleared room by room and street by street with the armour largely impotent as a result of the debris-strewn streets. The fighting was often hand-to-hand and there were heavy casualties on both sides. 2nd Glasgow Highlanders lost 12 officers and nearly 200 men on 26 June.

Stand A6: Le Haut du Bosq

DIRECTIONS: Continue along the D83 through the centre of Cheux heading south-west. Go over a crossroads, past a primary school on the right, past a water tower and up a gradual hill – this is le Haut du Bosq. It is easy to miss the village, but stop where

The hamlet of le Haut du Bosq. *(Author)*

A view from le Haut du Bosq back towards the start line on the extreme right flank of the VIII Corps attack. *(Author)*

you can and look around. A good place for this is a track on the right, approximately 200 metres after a sign showing that you have left Cheux and directly opposite a white sign on a green tubular stand. There is an excellent view to the north from this point.

THE ACTION: This village, which has changed little since 1944, was the objective of 9th Cameronians. The battalion and supporting armour had some 4,000 metres to traverse before they reached this position. 9th Cameronians, commanded by Lt-Col R.M. Villiers, advanced with A Company on the right, B Company on the left and C and D Companies to the rear, with the carrier platoon protecting the right flank. A Company met some stiff opposition from the outset and heavy casualties led to slow progress. B Company on the left was more fortunate and succeeded in overcoming several German posts concealed in the cornfields. Just like 2nd Glasgow Highlanders on the left, however, breaking the enemy's main line of resistance, including the minefield, was a costly business in terms of both time and casualties. II/26th SS Panzergrenadiers fought tenaciously to block 9th Cameronians' progress, while the 105-mm guns of *SS-Oberscharführer* (Sergeant-Major) Hans Hartmann's 5/12th SS Panzer Artillery, hit 9th Cameronians and 7th RTR hard from a distance of just over 3 km. The battalion was also held up by the fire that poured into it from the right flank as it approached le Haut du Bosq, as a result of 49th Division's failure to take the Rauray spur before Epsom began.

Wading through mines, hit on both flanks and encountering dug-

Men of 9th Cameronians in a sunken lane in le Haut du Bosq. The British infantry had to advance extremely cautiously as they entered villages for fear of snipers, booby traps, machine guns and tanks. *(IWM B5959)*

in opponents and snipers, the British infantry ploughed on to reach le Haut du Bosq at around 1100 hours. Here they found two batteries of I/12th SS Panzer Artillery and 26th SS Panzergrenadier Regiment headquarters, along with its specialist platoons. As 9th Cameronians approached the village over an open slope, it was engaged by anti-tank guns and machine guns and went to ground. At this point the supporting Churchills of 7th RTR and Crocodiles from 141st Regiment, RAC, were called forward and successfully created a breach in the defences that the infantry could exploit. Thus, by 1130 hours, the infantry had entered the northern part of the village and had begun clearing operations, which they had completed by midday. 9th Cameronians had suffered casualties of 6 officers and 120 men up to this point. Having secured the main part of le Haut du Bosq, the battalion spent the rest of the day trying to prise the Germans out of the woods on either side and the rising ground to the south, both of which were still strongly held.

15th Division still had battalions fighting in the four villages at noon on 26 June and fighting continued in and around them for the rest of the day with le Haut du Bosq and, in particular, Cheux, proving extremely difficult to take.

Stand A7: Rauray

DIRECTIONS: Continue on the D83 for just over 1 km to the crossroads and turn right on to the D139 towards Fontenay-le-Pesnel. After approximately 500 metres the road crosses Point 110 (modern maps shows the height as 120 metres); continue on to Rauray, a little further on. On entering the village, take the second turning on the right and pull over. The views of the northern part of the Epsom battlefield are excellent from here on a clear day.

A view from the Rauray spur looking back across the northern part of the Epsom battlefield. The church tower in Norrey-en-Bessin can just be seen on the right and le Mesnil-Patry is on the left. *(Author)*

Two Shermans from 24th Lancers, 8th Armoured Brigade, near Rauray on 29 June. The closer Sherman to the camera has an externally mounted .50-calibre machine gun. The German tank is an abandoned Panther. *(IWM B6226)*

THE ACTION: This is the important high ground that 49th Division of XXX Corps endeavoured to clear both before and during Operation Epsom. During the opening days of offensive, the Germans remained in possession of this area, which overlooks the northern part of the battlefield and gave the defenders a very great advantage. From 25 June, 49th Division edged its way forward towards this point. On the morning of 27 June, 11th DLI was on the northern outskirts of the village, trying to break in, supported by tanks of 1st Nottinghamshire (Sherwood Rangers) Yeomanry. III/26th SS Panzergrenadiers defended the village, with armour and 88-mm guns giving flanking fire. 1st Nottinghamshire Yeomanry lost several tanks trying to break in and eventually had to withdraw, leaving the infantry on their own. Gradually 11th DLI got a toehold into the village, the whole battalion suffering heavy casualties from mortar fire. In the late morning 11th DLI put in a battalion attack, bayonets fixed and in line abreast after a preliminary artillery barrage.

Corporal R.C. Baxter of No. 18 Platoon, D Company, 11th DLI, has said:

'The attack on Rauray was timed for 1100 hrs. "D" Company moved across a very flat field and were soon under fire from Spandaus. There was no cover at all and we could see the enemy quite clearly. After an attempt to advance further with help from our platoon mortars, a number of us were hit, including myself.'

Source: quoted in Kevin Baverstock, *Breaking the Panzers*, p. 39.

There were very heavy casualties and the attack failed. The attack was resumed at 1400 hours after a short ceasefire had been arranged for both sides to remove their wounded, and it was then that 11th DLI broke into the village, proceeding to mop it up during the afternoon. A vital piece of high ground had been taken, but the Germans still held the important positions of Brettevillette and Ring Contour 100, and it was to these that 49th Division then turned its attention.

TO CONCLUDE THE TOUR: Continue north-west along the D139, turn right on the D9 and follow the signs to Caen.

TO CONTINUE WITH TOUR B: Retrace your steps to Cheux. In the village, turn right onto the D89 and stop by the church.

TOUR B

THE ADVANCE TO THE TOURMAUVILLE BRIDGE

OBJECTIVE: A tour that traces 2nd Argylls' route from Cheux down through the Odon valley and examines the capture of the Tourmauville bridge and the establishment of a bridgehead there.

DURATION/SUITABILITY: Half a day if in a car. Suitable for cyclists and the disabled.

Stand B1: Cheux (south)

DIRECTIONS: Leave the N13 by the D83 and drive south for 5 km to Cheux. In the village turn left onto the D89 and park by the church. The church lies at the junction of the two critical roads running in a southerly direction out of the village towards the Odon. Most of the buildings in the area are either new or were heavily reconstructed after 1944.

Cheux church. This was a particularly dangerous area during the battle as the Germans had zeroed their guns on this landmark. *(Author)*

THE ACTION: This village was heavily damaged by the fighting and the debris caused by this made it extremely difficult for VIII Corps' units to move through. While 2nd Glasgow Highlanders fought in Cheux on the morning of 26 June, 7th Seaforths, 46th Brigade's reserve battalion, together with A Squadron, 7th RTR, moved up with the intention of pushing past the village and occupying Ring Contour 100 (roughly the area marked as le Gros Orme on the tour map on page 150). This important high ground was held by a mixture of panzergrenadiers and other arms who had been pushed back during the morning's fighting, and was

A Churchill tank of 7th RTR moving up to the front line on 25 June. The fact that this tank is from 7th RTR can be gleaned from the number '991' painted on the front. The number '40' is the bridge classification number, revealing that the tank weighs 40 tonnes. *(IWM B5993)*

reinforced just before 7th Seaforths reached it by men from 15th (Reconnaissance) Company of 25th SS Panzergrenadier Regiment. During its advance towards Cheux, 7th Seaforths came under heavy artillery fire. It was then further slowed by the attentions of the, as yet, uncleared German riflemen still scattered about the battlefield. Thus, when the men of the battalion reached Cheux they were late, fragmented and shaken.

> **Lieutenant James Hayter of 7th Seaforths later said:**
>
> 'When we finally reached Cheux we were few and minus our tanks. There was nothing to see but mud, water, ruins, smoke and mist and the air was alive with missiles...'
>
> Source: quoted in Tim Saunders, *Operation Epsom*, p. 60.

7th Seaforths then bypassed the ruined village to the east and began its attack on Point 100 at 1400 hours.

Stand B2: Ring Contour 100

DIRECTIONS: Take the D89 south-east past the church and stop at the fork in the road.

A view from the fork in the road on the D89 south of Cheux looking north. *(Author)*

THE ACTION: The D89 road, running in a south-easterly direction out of Cheux, was a critical route for VIII Corps' move down to Colleville and beyond. This route cuts across the high ground of Ring Contour 100, a valuable observation point that dominated the roads from Cheux to the Odon. It was, therefore, the scene of some considerable fighting.

On the D170 looking north across Ring Contour 100. *(Author)*

0
0.5
Kilometres
To N13
Cheux
POINT 100
(1944 maps)
To CAEN
le Champ Galop
la Fosse Pilon
Colleville
la Bruyère
Tourville-sur-Odon
le Haut de Tourville
Mondrainville
Grainville-sur-Odon
Baron-sur-Odon
Tourmauville
Gavrus
River Odon
B1
B2
B3
B4
B5
B6
B7
7th Seaforths
2nd Gordons
15/25th SS Panzergrenadiers
2nd Argylls
15th Division memorial
Base maps: IGN 1512OT,
IGN 1513E, IGN 1612OT

As soon as 7th Seaforths approached the Ring Contour, the Germans opened fire with multiple mortars and pinned the battalion down. After about half an hour there was a break in the bombardment and the battalion used this as an opportunity to continue its advance. As 7th Seaforths moved on to the high ground, however, it attracted fire from all directions and was bombarded by the German mortars once again. The battalion struggled forward and its B Company advanced to the crest of Ring Contour 100. Here its officer commanding, Major Robert L. Bickersteth, was killed and the supporting tanks suffered heavy losses. The southern slopes of the position were strongly held by the Germans and, with a murderous bombardment falling on 7th Seaforths, a decision was taken to withdraw slightly and dig in on the northern slopes. The battalion suffered 50 casualties that afternoon, and the supporting armour lost nine tanks.

Near the crest of Ring Contour 100, with Cheux ahead to the north and the water tower in le Haut du Bosq visible on the left. *(Author)*

Stand B3: Colleville

DIRECTIONS: Continue down the D89, crossing Ring Contour 100. After several hundred metres, the River Salbey will be crossed – barely a trickle of water in summer – and then the bridge spanning the A84, which has replaced the old railway line. Stop soon after crossing the bridge, on the wide, open bend by a ruined building. Your car can be left here while the village of Colleville is explored (a short walk down the D89a as shown by the sign-posts).

Men of 7th Seaforths attacking through a cornfield during Operation Epsom. *(IWM B5999)*

THE ACTION: Following up the morning attack by 44th and 46th Brigades was 227th Brigade. It was the task of 2nd Gordons to push south towards the Odon via Colleville, supported by C Squadron, 9th RTR. The battalion struggled gallantly with the armour to break into the village during the evening of 26 June, but was forced to withdraw, having suffered heavy casualties. Nevertheless, it was essential that Colleville was taken if progress was to be made down to the Odon and so another attack on the village was organised for the following morning. Thus, as 10th HLI ran into very solid German opposition south of le Haut du Bosq as it pushed for Grainville-sur-Odon, 2nd Argylls moved towards Colleville. The plan was for A and B Companies of 2nd Argylls to take Colleville and Tourville-sur-Odon, at which point C Company would push on and seize the bridge over the Odon (Tourmauville bridge), followed by B and D Companies, which would create a small bridgehead.

The position of 8/12th SS Panzers looking down towards Cheux. It was in this area that 10th HLI ran into the German tanks. *(Author)*

Major Ronnie Holden, officer commanding C Squadron, 9th RTR, on his view of the events of 26 June:

'H Hour arrived, and I gave the order to advance. At this point all hell was let loose, enemy artillery, nebelwerfers, anti-tank guns, tanks, the lot. Now immediately to our left after our start line was a 100 ring contour of high ground;

according to our original information this was to have been held by 15th Recce... in fact it was held by German panzers Marks III and IV. This caused heavy casualties on the Gordons and five of our tanks were put out of action. The original advance came to a temporary halt while a running battle was fought out between the squadron's left flank troops and these panzers. I fired off smoke to off-centre right in order to reform... Daylight was fading fast and fuel and ammunition were getting low... There remained only nine operational tanks of the squadron, with many wounded crews. This was the end of our first day in battle.'

Source: quoted in Peter Beale, *Tank Tracks*, p. 45.

2nd Argylls attacked towards the camera position through this area on the outskirts of Colleville. *(Author)*

2nd Argylls, commanded by Lt-Col John Tweedie and supported by B and C Squadrons, 23rd Hussars, had dug in just north of Cheux during the night of 26/27 June. Before dawn the battalion moved forward through a choked Cheux, passing the church as it made its way down the road to the start line on the eastern slopes of Ring Contour 100 (the area already passed on this tour). As they advanced towards Colleville, 2nd Argylls and 23rd Hussars encountered only light resistance. As A Company crossed the railway line, however, (just behind the ruined building at the stand) it ran into the first German defenders who, after a brief firefight, were overwhelmed. Meanwhile, B Company was held up by stubborn resistance in the village by men from 15/25th SS Panzer-grenadiers, 1st Battery of 53rd Anti-Aircraft Battalion, some members of 12th SS Panzer Division's supply chain and stragglers. The men of A Company pushed through the position where you are now standing and through some thick woods (the area is now much clearer), where they were heavily shelled and lost their direction. Thus the British attack was slowed and the advance on Tourville-sur-Odon lacked the cohesion and momentum that Tweedie would have liked. Nevertheless, with Colleville in British hands, VIII Corps at last had a foothold in the close country on the northern edge of the Odon valley.

Stand B4: Tourville-sur-Odon

DIRECTIONS: Continue down the D89 to Tourville. At the crossroads with the D675 Caen–Villers-Bocage road turn right and stop in the lay-by. The village has a bar, *le Tourville*.

The Caen–Villers-Bocage road at Tourville-sur-Odon. *(Author)*

THE ACTION: A and B Companies, 2nd Argylls, converged on this road but, as they had been fragmented while fighting through Colleville, they reached it only in dribs and drabs. B Company reached the road around where you are now, with A Company further to the west towards Mondrainville. This road was important to the Germans as a lateral route across the battlefield. Protected by machine guns in the village and patrolling armoured cars, German administrative transport was still using it as 2nd Argylls arrived. Thus, when the first section of B Company's lead platoon, commanded by Lieutenant Edwards, reached the road here, three or four of his men were immediately wounded. It was evident that the village needed to be cleared, which B Company then set about doing.

As B Company did so, what the battalion's war diary describes as 'two Tiger tanks' arrived. As Panzer IVs were often misidentified as Tigers, it is difficult to know whether these tanks really were Tigers. Nevertheless, whatever they were, they had had to be dealt with by 6-pounder anti-tank guns, which, luckily, were rushed up to B Company just in time. These guns were positioned with good fields of fire but were rather exposed, much to the chagrin of their commander, Lieutenant W. Muirhead. Nevertheless, his men were successful, destroying one of the tanks and forcing the other to flee. By this time both A and B Companies had consolidated a position on the road which, with the help of C Company, included Mondrainville, and set up a firm base for the battalion's attack to press onwards. At this point D Company moved forward and established itself on the high ground overlooking the Tourmauville bridge, while C Company moved down the road to the Odon.

Stand B5: The 15th Division memorial

DIRECTIONS: Go back to the crossroads and turn right on to the D89, heading down to the Odon. Note the exceptional views on leaving Tourville-sur-Odon across the Odon valley. After several hundred metres, stop by the memorial by the road on the right. This is the 15th Division memorial and is topped by a lion rampant growling towards the Odon and Hill 112.

THE ACTION: C Company advanced down this road towards the Odon, closely followed by B Company, with A Company holding Tourville (along with the carrier platoon and battalion headquarters) and with the flanks wide open. Although it could have been cut off, 2nd Argylls pushed on into valley in order to get to the Odon as quickly as possible – for it was only with the bridges in its possession that the next phase of Operation Epsom could begin.

Looking down the road from Tourville into the Odon valley. The 15th Division memorial is on the right where the road bends. *(Author)*

Stand B6: The Tourmauville bridge

DIRECTIONS: Continue down the road to the Tourmauville bridge. Note the dense countryside and the steepness of the road. Cross the bridge and park on the hard standing just beyond on the right.

Tourmauville bridge, a vital crossing point over the Odon to Hill 112. *(Author)*

The ground over which 2nd Argylls advanced to take the Tourmauville bridge, looking north from the north bank. *(Author)*

THE ACTION: The history of 2nd Argylls says: 'C Coy's dash to the bridge was probably the most classic manoeuvre carried out by the Battalion at any time during the campaign.' Commanded by Major Alan Fyfe, the company moved from copse to copse using archetypal fire and manoeuvre tactics with each platoon's move covered by another. Led by Fyfe, the final assault was made over open cornfields on the right side of the bridge and overwhelmed three machine-gun positions. The company took the bridge at 1700 hours with very few casualties and Fyfe was later awarded the Military Cross for this action. The bridge was taken intact; in a slick movement, C Company was quickly joined by D and B Companies and, a little later, by H Company of the motorised 8th Rifle Brigade from 29th Armoured Brigade. A crossing across the Odon had been achieved, but the troops there were at the point of a very narrow and vulnerable salient and it was critical for them to be reinforced as soon as possible. Accordingly, the Shermans of C Squadron, 23rd Hussars, were cheered when they arrived an hour or so later. 2nd Gordons arrived in Tourville-sur-Odon at 1900 hours and relieved A Company, 2nd Argylls, which then took over the defence of the bridge itself while the three other companies dug in beyond, creating a bridgehead some 200 metres in diameter. Signallers with the battalion then struggled (for some time unsuccessfully) to get a message out from their position in the close countryside to inform the brigade and division that the Tourmauville bridge (codenamed 'Quags') had been taken.

Stand B7: The Tourmauville bridgehead

DIRECTIONS: Continue on the D89 up through Tourmauville, climbing the steep Odon valley. Turn right at the crossroads on to the D214 towards Gavrus and pull over as soon as possible. Look north across the Odon valley.

THE ACTION: Once 23rd Hussars' C and B Squadrons had reached the bridge, they crossed, advanced through Tourmauville and fanned out on ground which gave a good field of fire. Meanwhile, 159th Brigade moved into the Odon valley to lend support to the vulnerable bridgehead. The brigade commander, Brigadier J.G. Sandie, organised this move poorly (and was replaced next day). His briefing to his battalion commanders was rushed – they did not even know what the general situation was, let alone whether the bridge had been taken. Thus, as the brigade set off towards the Odon as darkness fell, confusion reigned. 159th Brigade was then targeted by German mortars and artillery. Nevertheless, 4th KSLI on the left advanced through the night, in spite of having missed the supporting barrage, crossed the Odon and entered Baron-sur-Odon, and was well dug-in by dawn on 28 June.

> **Major Tim Ellis, officer commanding B Company, 4th KSLI, noted:**
>
> 'It was very dark among the trees and the maps were a trifle suspect. However, we crossed the river intact and just in time to meet the "moaning minnies" for the first time. B Company was sorting itself out in a field when these things arrived with their quite horrendous noise. The stonk seemed to fall all around us – the ground seemed to bounce up and down but nobody was hit.'
>
> *Source:* quoted in Patrick Delaforce, *The Black Bull*, p. 33.

On the right, 1st Herefords also crossed the Odon and took up positions around les Vilains. C Company of 3rd Monmouths got lost on its way to the bridge and ended up in Mouen where it stayed the night (and was caught up in the fierce fighting there the

A view from the Tourmauville bridgehead looking north over the valley to Tourville-sur-Odon and Mondrainville. *(Author)*

following morning), while the rest of the battalion took over the defence of the bridge from 2nd Argylls. The movement of 159th Brigade may have been poorly organised, but the bridgehead was strengthened by its arrival that night. Moreover, it allowed Lt-Col Tweedie to push the Argylls down towards Gavrus on the following afternoon (*see Tour D, pages 171–82*).

TO CONCLUDE THE TOUR: Return to the D89 and continue to the junction with the D8. Turn left and follow the signs to Caen.

TO CONTINUE WITH TOUR C: Turn the car round and follow the D214 into Baron-sur-Odon and stop by the church.

TOUR C

BARON-SUR-ODON – HILL 112 – HILL 113

OBJECTIVE: A tour that explores the critical high ground to the south of the River Odon, including Hills 112 and 113.

DURATION/SUITABILITY: Half a day if in a car. Suitable for cyclists. The tour is also suitable for the disabled, apart from Stand C3 (the Hill 112 woods).

Stand C1: Baron-sur-Odon

DIRECTIONS: From the Caen ring-road join the D675 (just south of the N175 junction) and after 750 metres fork left onto the D214. Follow this road for 5 km to Baron-sur-Odon. Park in the car park in front of the church. There is a memorial here to 227th Brigade's Brigadier Mackintosh-Walker who was killed nearby in July 1944.

THE ACTION: Baron-sur-Odon was secured by 4th KSLI on the evening of 27 June, and on the following morning the village was used as a launch pad for 29th Armoured Brigade's attack on Hill 112, to the south-east. The hill, topped by a broad plateau containing a small wood and orchard, was a critical point not only for Epsom, but also in Normandy as a whole, as it offered its occupants observation for kilometres in every direction.

The plaque outside the church in Baron-sur-Odon. *(Author)*

On the morning of 28 June, with the Germans quiet, 23rd Hussars sent its B Squadron from Baron-sur-Odon to the top of Hill 112 in order to probe the German defences. Approaching across Hill 112's northern slopes, 23rd Hussars' Shermans were engaged by guns in the vicinity of Fontaine-Étoupefour (2 km away to the north-east) and Château de Fontaine (2 km to the east); from the west by 88-mm guns from a motorised *Luftwaffe* anti-aircraft battery and some dug-in tanks in the woods around Esquay-Notre-Dame; and to their front by some other 88-mm guns and infantry positioned in the wood and orchard on the plateau.

Stand C2: The Hill 112 memorial

DIRECTIONS: Turn right out of the car park on to the D214 and after about 1.5 km the Baron-sur-Odon exit sign will come into view on the left, with a statue of the Madonna and Child on the

0.5
1
Kilometres
To CAEN
To GAVRUS
To BOUGY
River Odon
Baron-sur-Odon
Esquay-Notre-Dame
Evrecy
Avenay
Maizet
Gournay
la Bruyère
la Crête
Tourmauville
le Bon Repos
POINT 112 (1944 maps)
POINT 113 (1944 maps)
D214
D8
D89
D41
D36
D139
C1
C2
C3
C4
① 23rd Hussars
② F Company, 8th Rifle Brigade
③ German counter-attacks
④ 44th RTR
Base maps: IGN 1512OT, IGN 1513E, IGN 1612OT

The 43rd Division memorial on Hill 112. *(Author)*

opposite side of the road. Turn right here on to the Chemin Haussé, a long straight road leading to the Hill 112 memorial. The route that 23rd Hussars took up the northern slopes of Hill 112 on the morning of 28 June was parallel to this road but over to the right. At the top of the slope there is a crossroads, with the Hill 112 memorial across it on the left-hand side. Park up by the memorial. On the crossroads there is a battered Calvary as well as a memorial to 43rd Division. The Hill 112 memorial consists of a useful orientation table and a Churchill tank. Look in the direction of Baron-sur-Odon and the top of the church steeple can be seen, as can the area over which 23rd Hussars advanced. Esquay-Notre-Dame is over to the south-west, along with Hill 113, while to the south, down a track, are the woods that will be visited at the next stand. The wood that was on Hill 112 in June 1944 is the mass of trees to the left of this track.

The Churchill tank at the Hill 112 memorial. *(Author)*

THE ACTION: The men of 23rd Hussars did their best to destroy the guns and dug-in tanks that were their greatest cause for concern on Hill 112 and around Esquay-Notre-Dame, but they were unsuccessful. Their commanding officer called up some self-propelled anti-tank guns that were under command, but they also failed, as did a medium artillery bombardment. In the end, with the weather having cleared, rocket-firing Typhoons from 83 Group, RAF, were called, but the pilots had difficulty locating the Germans' positions, even when the tanks had marked them with red smoke. Meanwhile, 23rd Hussars' C Squadron and regimental headquarters were sent forward to reinforce B Squadron on the hill. With them was H Company, 8th Rifle Brigade, which had orders to clear the orchard and wood on the top.

A view from Hill 112 looking south-west towards Esquay-Notre-Dame and Hill 113. An utterly dominating feature as one can see from this photo! *(Author)*

Stand C3: The Hill 112 wood

DIRECTIONS: Take the track by the Hill 112 memorial car park down to the woods. The trees to the left of the track, the remains of a wood, are original while those to the right are more recently planted and have been made into a memorial park.

THE ACTION: The men of H Company, 8th Rifle Brigade, formed up in their transport in a wood at the eastern end of Baron-sur-Odon and advanced up the northern slope, past burning

23rd Hussars Shermans and then towards the orchard and wood. The hilltop was held by the equivalent of a company of panzergrenadiers from 12th SS Panzer Division who, along with some anti-tank gunners, fell back as the British infantry advanced on them. 8th Rifle Brigade's mortar platoon successfully advanced through the orchard and wood, with carrier sections on each flank, and the positions were taken. As H Company, 8th Rifle Brigade, dug in, 23rd Hussars was relieved on the hill by 3rd RTR and G Company, 8th Rifle Brigade, which moved up from Baron-sur-Odon through heavy tank fire. During 28 June, some 40 Shermans were lost on Hill 112. The British, although their position was extremely precarious, had taken the feature.

The newly-planted wood on Hill 112. The scars of battle can, however, still be seen. One veteran of the fighting told the author, 'It must be haunted'. *(Author)*

News that the British had taken Hill 112 quickly spread up the German chain of command and *SS-Obersturmbannführer* (Lt-Col) Max Wünsche, commander of 12th SS Panzer Regiment, launched a counter-attack. Some Panthers of I/12th SS Panzers attacked from the south and more Panthers and Panzer IVs of II/12th SS Panzers advanced up the hill from the south-west. The German armour adopted a wedge formation as it attacked and struck directly at the wooded area that 8th Rifle Brigade had just taken. Some British sections withdrew, but the remainder had enough anti-tank fire-power to repel the attack – but not before further Shermans were destroyed. The Germans may have failed in this attempt to dislodge

Looking south from the Hill 112 memorial towards the woods seized by 8th Rifle Brigade. *(Author)*

the British from the hill, but in this counter-attack and others that failed in a similar fashion later, they made it clear that any further movement forward by 29th Armoured Brigade would be met by armour and anti-tank guns.

Unable to remove the tanks and infantry from their positions on the Hill 112 plateau by armoured counter-attack, the Germans resorted to massive bombardments using every gun at their disposal. The intensity of the fire that the Germans laid down on the hill was something that nobody who witnessed it would ever forget.

8th Rifle Brigade's Trooper Roland Jefferson later commented:

'Hill 112 will always be remembered as our initiation into the real hatefulness of war. We found ourselves in a cornfield protecting the flanks overlooking the valley leading to Esquay.'

Major Noel Bell recalled that:

'All day long we had waited with every nerve alert for the expected counter-attack while shells and "minnies" rained down on us.'

29 June: Mechanised infantry of 8th Rifle Brigade pause from trench digging to be given mail and newspapers. *(IWM B6194)*

Rifleman Norman Habertin, 8th Rifle Brigade, vividly remembered the German bombardment:

'The storm broke. The enemy had been watching us settle down and before a single trench had been dug, down came those dreaded "moaning minnies". There was nothing to do but lie down and bite the earth. A half-track a few yards away went up in flames and when finally the mortaring stopped the complete battalion was in a state of utter chaos – all the company vehicles were mixed up, no one knew where their section or platoon was, wounded men were yelling for help and nobody in authority could get any orders carried out.'

Source: All quoted in Patrick Delaforce, *The Black Bull*, pp. 34–7.

At dusk the Germans mounted another counter-attack from Esquay-Notre-Dame with tanks supported by panzergrenadiers against the dazed and fatigued men of 29th Armoured Brigade. The British artillery tried to break up the thrust but failed and this time G Company, 8th Rifle Brigade, was forced to withdraw, thus surrendering the summit to the Germans once more. The deadly see-saw battle that Hill 112 eventually became famous for had begun.

View from the wood on Hill 112 down towards Esquay-Notre-Dame. *(Author)*

Stand C4: Hill 113

DIRECTIONS: Return to your car at the Hill 112 memorial and turn left towards Esquay-Notre-Dame (passing through le Bon Repos) on the D8. Continue onwards to Évrecy and stop where it is safe to do so at or near the roundabout on the eastern edge of the town. Point 113 was marked on 1944 maps a few hundred metres north of this stand (*see tour map, page 163*).

THE ACTION: On 29 June, while the infantry were busy tidying up the Scottish Corridor, 44th RTR, under the command of 29th Armoured Brigade, began an attack out of the western edge of the Odon bridgehead. Starting at 0700 hours, B Squadron, 44th RTR, moved on Évrecy, A Squadron to Esquay-Notre-Dame and C Squadron, supported by B Company, 2nd KRRC, attacked

Hill 113. Preparing for their own attack over the same ground, however, were elements of the newly-arrived II SS Panzer Corps. *SS-Obersturmführer* (Lieutenant) Franz Riedel, commander of 7/10th SS Panzer Regiment, had received orders to attack Hill 113 at 0700 hours that morning and then move on to Gavrus along with his regiment's 4th and 5th Companies. Moving from Bougy south-east towards Évrecy and Hill 113, Riedel ran into 44th RTR cutting across his front. The resulting exchange of fire saw the surprised British suffer at least ten Sherman tank losses and resulted in a swift, smoke-covered withdrawal, supported by the gunfire of 4th Royal Horse Artillery. After this 44th RTR remained on the defensive in the western portion of the Odon bridgehead for most of the day.

The action had stopped the British taking Hill 113, but it had also halted the first foray by II SS Panzer Corps towards the hill. This relatively brief battle, however, had wider implications, for 44th RTR's losses were quickly reported, making the British extremely wary about what was to come from the rest of II SS Panzer Corps.

Meanwhile, other German units struggled to establish themselves on Hill 113 throughout the day. Although they were eventually successful that evening, the battle had lasted so long that 10th SS Panzer Division's other planned attacks had to be postponed until the 30th.

One such attack was on Hill 112, for 3rd RTR, supported by H Company and one platoon of G Company, 8th Rifle Brigade, retook the plateau woods after a massive bombardment that morning. The ease with which this was achieved seems to have been due to a German mistake, in which the defending troops of 12th SS Panzer Division were withdrawn in anticipation of 10th SS Panzer Division's arrival. British occupation did not last for long, however, for, later on 29 June, 29th Armoured Brigade was ordered off Hill 112 to prepare for the expected II SS Panzer Corps counter-attacks.

TO CONCLUDE THE TOUR: Turn around in Évrecy, retracing your route along the D8 and follow the signs to Caen.

TO CONTINUE WITH TOUR D: Continue into Évrecy, and turn right on to the D174 to Bougy. In Bougy turn right on to the D214 and stop by the church.

Maj-Gen Roberts *(right)* with Brigadier Harvey (commander of 29th Armoured Brigade) by Roberts' command tank. *(IWM B9184)*

TOUR D

BOUGY AND GAVRUS

OBJECTIVE: A tour that examines 10th SS Panzer Division's counter-attack against the bridges over the Odon at Gavrus, held by 2nd Argylls, on 29 June.

DURATION/SUITABILITY: A couple of hours. Suitable for cyclists. The tour can be undertaken by the disabled, if the directions to walk to a point are undertaken by car.

Stand D1: Bougy Woods

DIRECTIONS: Follow the route given in Tour C from Caen to Baron-sur-Odon. Continue for another 4 km on the D214, through Gavrus to Bougy. Stop at Bougy church. 10th SS Panzer Division

To LE VALTRU &
GRAINVILLE-SUR-ODON
0
0.5
Kilometres
D 139
Cayer
le Moulin de Méhaye
Pont de Méhaye
River Odon
l'Odon
Gavrus
le Douet Paré
Cim.
Silo
les Bas Monceaux
Château de Bougy
Bougy
D 214
D139
D214
D174
D 174
RN
St. pomp.
Rvoir
D1
D2
D3
A
B
C
D
1 Approach by 2nd Argylls, 28 June
2 2nd Argylls, 29 June (company positions approximate)
3 Elements 10th SS Panzer division, 29 June
Base map: IGN 1513E

advanced through this village during its counter-attack on the afternoon of 29 June.

Bougy church. German troops advanced through this area on 29 June. *(Author)*

THE ACTION: On 29 June, II SS Panzer Corps massed for a major counter-attack into the south-western and western sectors of the Scottish Corridor while the British commanders, forewarned by intelligence, tried to regroup their assets to receive it. The British were slowed down in their efforts by horrendous traffic jams on the battlefield, whilst the Germans had to contend with harassment by Allied air power. Due to the clear conditions, the British forces were able to take advantage of their air superiority in a meaningful way for the first time in the battle. From dawn fighter-bombers went into action, and claimed to have destroyed or damaged over 100 German armoured and transport vehicles on 29 June. One battlegroup, consisting of III/20th SS Panzergrenadiers and the Panthers of I/9th SS Panzers, was moving to its assembly area at le Bas des Forges when German sources claim that it was attacked by approximately 100 Lancaster bombers. Twenty men were killed and a further 40 wounded, and some of the armoured vehicles were damaged. To make matters worse, 9th SS Panzer Division's tactical headquarters at les Novillons (known as les Nouillons in 1944) was also very badly damaged in another attack, making command and control of the division's assets extremely difficult. 10th SS Panzer Division was also targeted and there were attacks by rocket-firing Typhoons.

The view that the Germans had of Gavrus as they attacked from Bougy. *(Author)*

One junior German officer was *en route* for Bougy in a column of Panthers when one such strike took place:

'The German soldier feared the good weather as he knew that British aircraft would use it to spot movements on the ground and then target them. This happened to us on the morning of 29 June as we were approaching our assembly point. The noise of our own engines masked the sound of the approaching aircraft and we did not see them until it was too late. The Typhoon pilots were extremely skilled and seemed to target command vehicles rather than just firing indiscriminately. Their rockets destroyed everything in their way and then their cannon sliced into what was left. The attack was over in minutes, before we had a chance to react, but the result was devastation.'

Source: Author's interview with former *SS-Obersturmführer* (Lt) Ernst Steiner, a Panther commander.

The result of these British air attacks was to disrupt certain German units and severely upset the plans of the divisions and the corps.

A soldier, bayonet fixed on his No. 4 Mark I .303 Lee Enfield, waits in a field for the advance to continue on the afternoon of 26 June. *(IWM B5958)*

As *SS-Obergruppenführer* (Lt-Gen) Paul Hausser later confirmed, the attack:

'...was scheduled to begin at seven o'clock in the morning but hardly had the tanks assembled when they were attacked by fighter-bombers. This disrupted the troops so much that the attack did not start again till two-thirty in the afternoon. But even then it could not get going. The murderous fire from naval guns in the Channel and the terrible British artillery destroyed the bulk of our attacking force in its assembly area.'

Source: quoted in L.F. Ellis, *Victory in the West*, p. 284.

Other commanders went as far to say that the disruption to their preparations meant that the counter-attacks had failed before they had even begun, but others insist that the impact of the British raids and bombardments was merely used to excuse failure. What is without doubt, however, is that on the morning of 29 June, the British did severely disrupt the German counter-attack preparations.

II SS Panzer Corps had assembled around 250 tanks and assault guns for the attack and its plans were unchanged by Bittrich in spite of the delay. 9th SS Panzer Division was to attack north of the Odon in the vicinity of Grainville-sur-Odon, cut the corridor and then link up with 12th SS Panzer Division at Carpiquet airfield. 10th SS Panzer Division was to attack to the south of the Odon, and, having taken Hill 113 on the morning of 29 June, push on to Hill 112 and then drive into the Tourmauville bridgehead. Meanwhile, elements of 12th SS Panzer Division and Battlegroup *Frey* were to exert some pressure on the eastern and south-eastern flanks of the Scottish Corridor.

To the west of Bougy, 21st SS Panzergrenadier Regiment, supported by self-propelled guns of 7/ and 8/10th SS Panzer Regiment, formed up on the morning of 29 June in preparation to lead 10th SS Panzer Division's attack against the Gavrus bridges. At about 1500 hours these troops passed through Bougy and 50 minutes later, 29th Armoured Brigade reported to 11th Armoured Division that German tanks and infantry were attacking Gavrus.

Bougy Woods, where the panzergrenadiers of 10th SS Panzer Division formed up for their attack on Gavrus. *(Author)*

Stand D2: The bridges at Gavrus

DIRECTIONS: Follow the D214 sign to Gavrus, continue to the crossroads and turn left. Continue down to the bridges over the Odon, cross both bridges (the Odon here has two channels) and pull in on the left just after the second bridge.

A view of the Gavrus bridges. The bridge closer to the camera position is the northern crossing. *(Author)*

THE ACTION: The bridges at Gavrus were captured after Lt-Col Tweedie, commanding officer of 2nd Argylls, sent two platoon-strength fighting patrols, one from A Company and the second from B Company, down the banks of the Odon from the Tourmauville bridge during the afternoon of 28 June. Both patrols had reported to the battalion by radio by 1600 hours that, once again, they had taken the bridges unopposed and intact. As soon as these messages were received, Tweedie sent C Company to reinforce the two platoons, but shortly after he was ordered to send the entire battalion across to Gavrus. The route that 2nd Argylls took was along the extremely difficult wooded and marshy southern bank of the Odon, where the movement of the 6-pounder anti-tank guns was particularly problematical. During this time, had the Germans ambushed the battalion, the results would have been devastating; luckily for Tweedie this did not happen, and the battalion arrived complete at Gavrus before dark.

The location of the two bridges over the separate channels of the Odon and the surrounding terrain reveal to this day what a difficult place this was to hold for a single battalion, particularly one so completely isolated. Nevertheless, two companies were immediately sent south of the river, C Company digging in on the right from the river bank to the road while A Company took up a position on the left in a wood on a steep slope. Then, after it had been confirmed that Gavrus was devoid of the enemy, B Company was positioned astride the road forward of the other two companies, in some buildings. Battalion headquarters remained on the north bank of the Odon in a quarry, with D Company adjacent, and the carrier platoon dug in to the west of the northern bridge. The night of 28/29 June was quiet, as was the following morning.

Stand D3: Gavrus

DIRECTIONS: Walk back over the bridges and back into Gavrus to explore. The car can be taken if necessary, of course, but walking provides a better sense of this difficult ground.

Elements of 10th SS Panzer Division moved into this area of Gavrus on 29 June. *(Author)*

The area of Gavrus defended by B Company, 2nd Argylls, taken towards the northern end of the village looking north. *(Author)*

THE ACTION: On the morning of 29 June, 2nd Argylls sent out patrols to reconnoitre the ground to its front and found some patrols from 8th Rifle Brigade at the crossroads at the top of the village. However, at a little after 1500 hours that afternoon, 10th SS Panzer Division launched its counter-attack, led by 21st SS Panzergrenadier Regiment, from the direction of Bougy. The German attack lasted for five hours and was characterised for most of this period by infantry assaults on B Company, to the west of the road. As a result of this pressure, and some heavy artillery and mortar bombardments, the men of B Company were in the thick of the action. Although suffering heavy casualties, they did not concede any ground and there was no fear of them being overrun.

In such circumstances, questions have to be asked about the strength of the German attack on Gavrus and the way in which it was conducted. During the German push, there was an attempt to try and outflank B Company's position to the west, but this merely meant that the panzergrenadiers ran into C Company. It was not until the evening that the Germans brought up some armour, which allowed Tweedie time to position his anti-tank guns and PIATs carefully. The armour, probably two Panzer IVs (although there were reports that they were Tigers), came down the road towards the bridges. One was knocked out by a 6-pounder and the other was stopped by a PIAT, manned by Corporal Stewart of B Company.

Using another PIAT, Captain Mackenzie, second-in-command of B Company, took on three other tanks that tried to attack through the hedges along the Bougy to Gavrus road, and forced them to withdraw. Thus far only B and C Companies had been engaged and, greatly assisted by the accurate and timely supporting fire by 495th Field Battery, RA, they had stopped the Germans.

Even so, as the day progressed, the Germans did begin to infiltrate between some of the companies' sections. One such penetration into C Company's positions down a sunken lane came in behind B Company's No. 11 Platoon. This was soon spotted, and although it was difficult for the platoon to wriggle out of the envelopment, it held on. Sensing the difficulties being faced on the right flank, A Company on the left sent a platoon across the road in order to counter-attack and recover the sunken lane, but the platoon became pinned down at the side of the road by German machine-gun fire before it could attack. In another attempt to alleviate the situation, B Company's officer commanding, Major W.L. McElwee, ordered his uncommitted No. 10 Platoon from the east side of the road back down towards the southern bridge, to cross the road and then move into C Company's sector. This move left the defence of the east flank in the sole hands of A Company at the bridge, but in the circumstances it was a risk worth taking. No. 10 Platoon's attack across the road failed, however, once again the victim of heavy machine-gun fire from some high ground to the west of the village.

Thus, Major Fyfe, commanding C Company and senior officer on the spot, decided to move his company and the remnants of B Company back across the road and into the position held by A Company. From this position, he decided, the approaches to the bridge could still be commanded. It took approximately an hour for this movement to take place and the battalion's situation improved markedly as a result. The problem by this stage, however, was that ammunition was running low and it took a feat of great bravery on the part of CSM Davies to get across the two bridges and, under fire, drive back D Company's carrier full of ammunition. By this time there were approximately 100 men of A Company, 30 of B Company and 40 of C Company in the woods by the bridge. Major Fyfe himself had actually been cut off as he tried to round up the last of his men and was forced to make his way back to the battalion via the Tourmauville bridge. By 2000 hours the German attacks had petered out; the men of 2nd Argylls breathed a collective sigh of relief, and the wounded were evacuated back across the river.

The area defended by A Company, 2nd Argylls, to the east of the southern Gavrus bridge. *(Author)*

The night of 29/30 June was quiet for the remnants of the battalion, but Tweedie's men remained isolated. In the late morning of 30 June the Germans tentatively began to probe Gavrus again, covered by an artillery and mortar bombardment directed by observers on the high ground towards Bougy. The counter-attack that followed began at 1500 hours but was fragmented by the British artillery, even though communication had initially broken down after the radio linking 2nd Argylls to the field battery had been destroyed. This problem was overcome by a new radio set being brought forward, but when the radio linking the battalion to 227th Brigade and 2nd Argylls' headquarters with the companies was also destroyed, there were no such replacements. Thus, the battalion became more isolated than ever and its companies completely detached from Tweedie's command.

Some British tanks did arrive in the battalion area from the north, but they were not to be deployed to lend support at the bridges, merely to facilitate the battalion's withdrawal back to the brigade position at Colleville. With communications with the rest of the battalion down, however, only D Company and the battalion headquarters withdrew – but without Tweedie. Prior to the arrival of the tanks Tweedie and two other officers had, because of the communication breakdown, tried to make personal contact with the men at the bridges but had become pinned down in some woods before they got there. While this small group sheltered in the woods, news of the withdrawal reached the three companies at the bridges and at 2130 hours they pulled back. It was not until the following day that Tweedie was found and he, too, made his way back to a reunion with his battalion.

Rifleman Brett from Newport, Isle of Wight, takes cover beneath a jeep. He is armed with a Mark III Sten gun. *(IWM B5998)*

Operation Epsom had been an outstanding success for 2nd Argylls even if the operation itself had not worked out as planned. Having seized three bridges intact and having defended the Gavrus bridges on its own against the attention of 10th SS Panzer Division for two days, 2nd Argylls had done all that was asked of it – and considerably more. The battalion's casualties were one officer and 32 other ranks dead and six officers and approximately 150 other ranks wounded or missing.

TO CONCLUDE THE TOUR: Continue north on the D139 and then turn right on to the D675 to Caen.

PART FOUR

ON YOUR RETURN

FURTHER RESEARCH

A visit to the Operation Epsom battlefield may well kindle in you a desire to learn more about the battle and to engage in research about the formations and units involved. If this is the case then there are many museums that can provide information. These include: the *Imperial War Museum*, *Firepower – The New Royal Artillery Experience*, the *National Army Museum*, and the *Tank Museum*. There were too many regiments involved in Operation Epsom to list the contact details of each here. However, the following address will provide all of the necessary information: <www.army.mod.uk/ceremonialandheritage/museums_main.htm>.

Useful Addresses

UK National Archives, Public Record Office, Kew, Richmond, Surrey TW9 4DU; tel: 020 8876 3444; email: <enquiry@nationalarchives.gov.uk>; web: <www.nationalarchives.gov.uk>.

Imperial War Museum, Lambeth Road, London SE1 6HZ; tel: 020 7416 5320; email: <mail@iwm.org.uk>; web: <www.iwm.org.uk>.

British Library, 96 Euston Road, London NW1 2DB; tel: 020 7412 7676; <email: reader-services-enquiries@bl.uk>.

University of Keele Air Photo Library, Keele University, Keele, Staffordshire ST5 5BG; tel/fax: 01782 583395; web: <evidenceincamera.co.uk>.

Firepower – The New Royal Artillery Experience, Woolwich, London; tel: 0208 855 7755.

National Army Museum, Royal Hospital Road, London SW3 4HT; tel: 020 7730 0717; web: <www.national-army-museum.ac.uk>.

Tank Museum, Bovington, Dorset BH20 6JG; tel: 01929 405096; web: <www.tankmuseum.co.uk>.

There has been little written specifically about Operation Epsom, although most books on the Battle of Normandy refer to it. Nevertheless, the following are useful, though not all are still in print and some may only be available from specialist libraries or by inter-library loan.

Above: The view over the Epsom battlefield towards Caen from the summit of Hill 112. *(Author)*

Page 183: Despatch riders from 15th (Scottish) Division approaching the front line on 25 June. The '60' on the side of the BSA M20 motorcycle denotes that this rider is attached to one of the infantry battalions. *(IWM B5991)*

BIBLIOGRAPHY

Barclay, C.N., *The History of the Cameronians (Scottish Rifles)*, Volume III, *1933–1946*, Sifton Praed, no date given

Baverstock, Kevin, *Breaking the Panzers – The Bloody Battle for Rauray, Normandy 1 July 1944*, Sutton Publishing, 2002

Baynes, John, *The Forgotten Victor – General Sir Richard O'Connor*, Brassey's, 1989

Beale, Peter, *Tank Tracks – 9th Battalion Royal Tank Regiment at War 1940–45*, Alan Sutton Publishing, 1995

Brisset, Jean, *The Charge of the Bull – The Battles of 11th British Armoured Division for the Liberation of the Bocage*, Bates Books, 1989

D'Este, Carlo, *Decision In Normandy*, Pan Books, 1984

Delaforce, Patrick, *The Black Bull – From Normandy to the Baltic with 11th Armoured Division*, Alan Sutton Publishing, 1993

Ellis, L.F. *et. al.*, *Victory In The West*, Volume I, *The Battle of Normandy*, HMSO, 1962

Hamilton, Nigel, *Monty: Master of the Battlefield 1942–44*, Hamish Hamilton, 1983

The steep and wooded banks of the Odon, as seen from the Tourmauville bridge. Although the river itself is modest in size its valley was a substantial obstacle to vehicle movement *(Author)*

Hastings, R.H.W.S., *The Rifle Brigade in the Second World War 1939–45*, Gale and Polden, 1950

Horne, Alistair (with David Montgomery), *Monty – The Lonely Leader, 1944–1945*, Macmillan, 1994

Keegan, John, *Six Armies in Normandy*, Penguin, 1982

Lehmann, Rudolf, and Tiemann, Ralf, *The Leibstandarte*, Vol. 4, Pt. 1, J.J. Fedorowicz, 1993

Luther, Craig W.H., *Blood and Honor: The History of the 12th SS Panzer Division 'Hitler Youth', 1943–45*, R. James Bender Publishing, 1987

Martin, H.G., *The History of the Fifteenth Scottish Division 1939–1945*, William Blackwood and Sons, 1948

McBain, S.W. (ed.), *A Regiment At War – The Royal Scots (The Royal Regiment) 1939–45*, The Pentland Press, 1988

McElwee, W.L., *History of the Argyll and Sutherland Highlanders 2nd Battalion – European Campaign 1944–45*, no publisher given, 1949

Meyer, Herbert, *The History of the 12. SS-Panzerdivision Hitlerjugend*, J.J. Fedorowicz Publishing, 1994

Meyer, Kurt, *Grenadiers*, J.J. Fedorowicz Publishing, 1994

Miles, Wilfred, *The Life of a Regiment* , Volume V, *The Gordon Highlanders 1919–45*, Frederick Warne, 1980

Neillands, Robin, *The Battle of Normandy 1944*, Cassell, 2003

Perrigault, Jean-Claude, *21. Panzerdivision*, Heimdal, 2002

Reynolds, Michael, *Sons of the Reich – II SS Panzer Corps*, Spellmount, 2002

Reynolds, Michael, *Steel Inferno – I SS Panzer Corps in Normandy*, Spellmount, 1997

Saunders, Tim, *Hill 112*, Leo Cooper, 2001

Saunders, Tim, *Operation Epsom*, Leo Cooper, 2003

Sym, John (ed.), *Seaforth Highlanders*, Gale and Polden, 1962

Tieke, Wilhelm, *In The Firestorm of the Last Years of the War – II SS Panzerkorps With The 9. and 10. SS-Divisions 'Hohenstaufen' and 'Frundsberg'*, J.J. Fedorowicz, 1999

3 July: A corner of Cheux, illustrating both the effects of the unseasonal wet weather and the sort of damage that the battle inflicted on the villages in the area. Note also the German direction signs still nailed to the tree. *(IWM B6322)*

The Argyll and Sutherland Highlanders' cap badge, as worn by 2nd Argylls during Operation Epsom. *(IWM H25656)*

PRIMARY SOURCES

Primary source documents relating to the planning and execution of Operation Epsom can be found at the National Archives (formerly known as the Public Record Office) at Kew. The following are just a small selection of those that are relevant (with the classification numbers showing where they can be found):

VIII Corps – WO171/286; 15th (Scottish) Division – WO171/466; 43rd Division – WO171/479; 11th Armoured Division – WO171/456; 4th Armoured Brigade – WO171/601; 31st Tank Brigade – WO171/633; 29th Armoured Brigade – WO171/627; 44th Brigade – WO171/646; 46th Brigade – WO171/648; 129th Brigade – WO171/658; 130th Brigade – WO171/660; 159th Brigade – WO171/691; 214th Brigade – WO171/708; 227th Brigade – WO171/712; 2nd Argylls – WO171/1262; 9th Cameronians – WO171/1277; 5th DCLI – WO171/1280; 2nd Glasgow Highlanders – WO171/1297; 2nd Gordons – WO171/1300; Hallamshire Battalion – WO171/1305; 10th HLI – WO171/1313; 6th KOSB – WO171/1322; 12th KRRC – WO171/1328; 4th Lincolns – WO171/1335; 3rd Monmouths – WO171/1349; 8th Rifle Brigade – WO171/1359; 8th Royal Scots – WO171/1362; 6th RSF – WO171/1364; 7th Seaforths – WO171/1371; 4th Somersets – WO171/1372; 7th Somersets– WO171/1373; 4th Wiltshires – WO171/1394; 5th Wiltshires – WO171/1395; 1st Worcesters – WO171/1396; 2nd Fife and Forfar Yeomanry – WO171/853; 3rd County of London Yeomanry – WO171/855; 4th County of London Yeomanry – WO171/856; 2nd Northamptonshire Yeomanry – WO171/860; 3rd RTR – WO171/866; 7th RTR – WO171/868; 9th RTR – WO171/869; 44th RTR – WO171/873; Royal Scots Greys – WO171/842; 4th/7th Royal Dragoon Guards – WO171/838; 23rd Hussars – WO171/847; 24th Lancers – WO171/848.

INDEX

Page numbers in *italics* denote an illustration.